Debbie Bliss

Nursery Knits

Debbie Bliss
Nursery Knits

More than 30 designs for clothes, toys and other items for 0–3 year olds

St. Martin's Griffin
New York

For Barry, Billy and Eleanor

Library of Congress Cataloging-in-Publication Data available on request.

ISBN 0-312-14584-5

First St Martin's Griffin Edtion: October 1996
10 9 8 7 6 5 4 3 2

First published in the United Kingdom in 1996 by Ebury Press Random House, 20 Vauxhall Bridge Road, London SW1V 2SA

Photography by Sandra Lousada
Designed by Jerry Goldie Graphic Design
Styling by Marie Willey

Printed and bound in Italy by New Interlitho Italia, S.p.a., Milan

ALSO BY DEBBIE BLISS
Baby Knits
New Baby Knits
Kid's Country Knits
Kid's Knits for Heads, Hands and Toes
Toy Knits

Contents

Introduction

My latest collection of knits for children was inspired by images of childhood from days gone by - a time of rocking horses and sailing boats, dolls' houses and skipping ropes. I have tried to recreate this period not only by using these motifs but also by working with a soft palette of 'nursery' shades - cream and primrose, dusky blues, lilacs and pinks, with subtly flecked tweeds. Some of the designs for small babies are updated versions of the old-fashioned layette and many of the garments have matching accessories, such as bootees or a blanket. Other outfits are accompanied by a toy, such as a small sailor bear with the classic sailor top or a tiny sheep that can be popped into the pocket of the smock.

The designs cover ages from 3 months to 3 years and range from the simple to the more challenging to meet the needs of a variety of knitting abilities.

Basic Information

NOTES

Figures for larger sizes are given in ( ) brackets. Where only one figure appears, this applies to all sizes.

Work figures given in [ ] the number of times stated afterwards.

Where 0 appears no stitches or rows are worked for this size.

YARNS

All amounts are based on average requirements and should therefore be regarded as approximate. It is always best to use the yarn recommended in the knitting pattern instructions. Addresses for Rowan Yarns are given on page 80. If, however, you cannot find the yarn specified, you can substitute a yarn of similar weight and type. The descriptions of the various Rowan yarns are meant as a guide to the yarn weight and type (i.e. cotton, wool, et cetera). Remember that the description of the yarn weight is only a guide and you should test a yarn first to see if it will achieve the correct tensions (gauge).

The amount of substitute yarn needed is determined by the number of metres (yards) required rather than by the number of grammes (ounces). If you are unsure when choosing a suitable substitute, ask the assistant at your yarn shop to assist you.

Description of Rowan Yarns

Cotton Glace - a lightweight cotton yarn (100% cotton) approx 112m (123yd) per 50g (1¾oz) ball

Designer DK - a double knitting (US worsted) weight yarn (100% pure new wool) approx 115m (125yd) per 50g 1¾oz) ball

Handknit DK Cotton - a medium weight cotton yarn (100% cotton) approx 85m (90yd) per 50g (1¾oz) ball

True 4 ply Botany - a 4 ply yarn (100% pure new wool) approx 170m (220yd) per 50g (1¾oz) ball

Recycled Chunky - a chunky weight yarn (100% pure new wool) approx 100m (109yd) per 100g (3¾oz) hank

DK Tweed - a double knitting weight yarn (100% pure new wool) approx 110m (143yd) per 50g (1¾oz) hank

TENSION

Tension is the number of stitches and rows per centimetre (inch) that should be obtained on given needles, yarn and stitch pattern. To check your tension, knit a sample at least 12.5 x 12.5cm (5in) square, using the same yarn, needles and stitch pattern as those to be used for main work. Smooth out the finished sample on a flat surface but do not stretch it. With a ruler, mark out a 10cm (4in) square with pins. Count the number of stitches and rows between pins. If the number of stitches and rows is greater than specified try again using larger needles; if less use smaller needles.

Tension is not as crucial when knitting toys as it would be for other knitted garments. A tighter or looser tension will produce a smaller or larger toy than that shown in the photograph, and a loose tension will produce a more open fabric through which the stuffing will show or come through.

STUFFING

Overstuffing stretches the fabric so that the stuffing shows through and understuffing makes the toy too floppy. Watch out for 'lumps' when stuffing. Tear the edges of each piece of stuffing so that the edges blend in when inserted.

SAFETY

It is very important that a toy is suitable for the age of the child for whom it is intended. Toys given to children under 3 years of age should not have any added extras such as buttons or eyes which could become loose. Make sure that any toys given to the very young have all limbs and any accessories securely sewn in place. Washable stuffing, which conforms to safety standards, should always be used and yarns should be either 100% wool or 100% cotton.

Abbreviations

alt=alternate
beg=begin(ning)
cont=continue
dec=decreas(e)ing
foll=following
inc=increas(e)ing
k=knit
m1=make one by picking up loop lying between st just worked and next st and work into the back of it
patt=pattern
p=purl
psso=pass slipped stitch over
rem=remain(ing)
rep=repeat
sl=slip
skpo=slip 1, k1, pass slipped st over
st(s)=stitch(es)
st st=stocking stitch
tbl=through back of loop(s)
tog=together
yb=yarn back
yf=yarn forward
yon=yarn over needle
yrn=yarn round needle

Smock with Sheep

SEE PAGE
47

12
*Tartan All-in-One
with Patchwork
Blanket and
Gingham Bear*

SEE PAGE
41

13

CLOCKWISE, FROM LEFT
Rosebud Shoes,
Smock Shoes,
Fair Isle Shoes,
Teddy with
Dress, Rosebud
Teddy
SEE PAGES
55, 47, 52

All-in-One with Bootees, Hat and Rabbit

SEE PAGE
44

18

Nursery Cardigan

SEE PAGE
50

19

CLOCKWISE, FROM LEFT

Rosebud Blanket, ABC Blanket,
Smock, Nursery Cardigan

SEE PAGES
55, 60, 47, 50

Bunny and Chick Jacket

SEE PAGE
49

**Fair Isle Ballet Top
with Shoes and
Teddy with Dress**

SEE PAGE
52

22

*Rosebud Cardigan,
Shoes, Blanket
and Teddy*

SEE PAGE

55

23
Twinset with
Fair Isle Border

SEE PAGE
58

24

**Fair Isle
Ballet Top with
Shoes and
Teddy with
Dress**

SEE PAGE
52

25
Cardigan with
Fair Isle Border

SEE PAGE
58

26
ABC Sweater

SEE PAGE
60

27

**Bo Peep Sweater
and ABC Blanket**

SEE PAGES
62, 60

28

Duck Jacket

SEE PAGE
64

*Sailor Top
with Teddy*

SEE PAGE
65

30
*Jacket with
Sampler Panels*

SEE PAGE
67

31
Toy Sweater

SEE PAGE
69

32

Coat with Contrast Lining

SEE PAGE
71

33
Moss Stitch and
Cable Waistcoat

SEE PAGE
73

Ducks and
Boats Sweater

SEE PAGE
76

35
*Cardigan with Lace
Edging*
SEE PAGE
74

36
*Cable
Jacket
and Beret*

SEE PAGE
77

37
Cable Coat with Hat

SEE PAGE
78

Bunny and Chick Jacket

SEE PAGE
49

Teddy All-in-One

See Pages
10/11

MATERIALS
7(8: 9) 50g balls of Rowan Designer DK Wool in Beige (A).
1 ball of same in Brown (B).
Pair each of 3¼mm (No 10/US 3) and 4mm (No 8/US 6) knitting needles.
11 buttons.

TENSION
22 sts and 44 rows to 10cm/4in square over garter st (every row k) on 4mm (No 8/US 6) needles.

ABBREVIATIONS
See page 7.

MEASUREMENTS

To fit age	3	6	9	months
Actual chest	53	56	59	cm
measurement	21	22	23¼	in
Length from beginning	44	48	52	cm
of leg cuff to back neck	17¼	19	20½	in
Inside leg seam	9	11	13	cm
	3½	4¼	5	in
Sleeve seam	14	16	18	cm
	5½	6¼	7	in

LEFT FOOT
With 4mm (No 8/US 6) needles and A, cast on 32(34: 36) sts.
1st row and 4 foll alt rows (right side) K.
2nd row [K13(14: 15), m1, k1, m1, k2] twice.
4th row [K13(14: 15), m1, k3, m1, k2] twice.
6th row [K13(14: 15), m1, k5, m1, k2] twice.
8th row [K13(14: 15), m1, k7, m1, k2] twice.
10th row [K13(14: 15), m1, k9, m1, k2] twice. 52(54: 56) sts.
11th to 15th rows K.
16th row K13(14: 15), k2 tog tbl, k7, k2 tog, k to end.
17th to 19th rows K.
20th row K13(14: 15), k2 tog tbl, k5, k2 tog, k to end.
21st to 23rd rows K.
24th row K13(14: 15), k2 tog tbl, k3, k2 tog, k to end.
25th row and 4 foll alt rows K.
26th row K12(13: 14), k2 tog tbl, k3, k2 tog, k to end.
28th row K11(12: 13), k2 tog tbl, k3, k2 tog, k to end.
30th row K10(11: 12), k2 tog tbl, k3, k2 tog, k to end.
32nd row K9(10: 11), k2 tog tbl, k3, k2 tog, k to end.
34th row K8(9: 10), k2 tog tbl, k3, k2 tog, k to end. 36(38: 40) sts. K 1 row.
Left Leg
** Change to 3¼mm (No 10/US 3) needles.
Next row (wrong side) *[K1, p1] twice, [k1, p1] all in next st; rep from * to last 1(3: 5) sts, [k1, p1] 0(1: 2) times, k1. 43(45: 47) sts.
1st rib row P1, [k1, p1] to end.
2nd rib row K1, [p1, k1] to end.
Rib 3 rows more.
Next row Rib 3(3: 2), [m1, rib 1, m1, rib 2] 13(13: 14) times, [m1, rib 2] 0(1: 1) time, rib 1. 69(72: 76) sts.
Change to 4mm (No 8/US 6) needles.
Cont in garter st until work measures 9(11: 13)cm/3½(4¼: 5)in from beg of rib, ending with a wrong side row.
Shape Crotch
Cast off 3 sts at beg of next 2 rows.
Dec one st at beg of next 4 rows. **
Leave rem 59(62: 66) sts on a holder.

RIGHT FOOT
With 4mm (No 8/US 6) needles and A, cast on 32(34: 36) sts.
1st row and 4 foll alt rows (right side) K.
2nd row [K2, m1, k1, m1, k13(14: 15)] twice.
4th row [K2, m1, k3, m1, k13(14: 15)] twice.
6th row [K2, m1, k5, m1, k13(14: 15)] twice.
8th row [K2, m1, k7, m1, k13(14: 15)] twice.
10th row [K2, m1, k9, m1, k13(14: 15)] twice. 52(54: 56) sts.
11th to 15th rows K.
16th row K28(29: 30), k2 tog tbl, k7, k2 tog, k to end.
17th to 19th rows K.
20th row K28(29: 30), k2 tog tbl, k5, k2 tog, k to end.
21st to 23rd rows K.
24th row K28(29: 30), k2 tog tbl, k3, k2 tog, k to end.
25th row and 4 foll alt rows K.
26th row K27(28: 29), k2 tog tbl, k3, k2 tog, k to end.
28th row K26(27: 28), k2 tog tbl, k3, k2 tog, k to end.
30th row K25(26: 27), k2 tog tbl, k3, k2 tog, k to end.
32nd row K24(25: 26), k2 tog tbl, k3, k2 tog, k to end.
34th row K23(24: 25), k2 tog tbl, k3, k2 tog, k to end. 36(38: 40) sts.
K 1 row.
Right Leg
Work as given for Left Leg from ** to **.
Body
Next row K to end, then k across sts of Left Leg. 118(124: 132) sts.
Work a further 3cm/1¼in in garter st, ending with a wrong side row.
Shape Front Opening
Cast off 3 sts at beg of next 2 rows. 112(118: 126) sts. Cont straight until work measures 30(33: 36)cm/11¾(13: 14¼)in from beg of rib, ending with a wrong side row.
Right Front
Next row K26(28: 30), turn.
Work on this set of sts only for a further 9(10: 11)cm/3½(4: 4¼)in, ending with a wrong side row.
Shape Neck
Cast off 3 sts at beg of next row. Dec one st at neck edge on every row until 19(20: 21) sts rem. Cont straight until work measures 44(48: 52)cm/17¼(19: 20½)in from beg of rib, ending with a right side row.
Shape Shoulder
Cast off 10(10: 11) sts at beg of next row. K 1 row. Cast off rem sts.
Back
With right side facing, rejoin yarn to rem sts and k60(62: 66) sts, turn.
Work on this set of sts only until Back matches Right Front to shoulder, ending with a wrong side row.
Shape Shoulders
Cast off 10(10: 11) sts at beg of next 2 rows and 9(10: 10) sts at beg of foll 2 rows. Leave rem 22(22: 24) sts on a holder.
Left Front
With right side facing, rejoin yarn to rem 26(28: 30) sts and k to end.
Complete to match Right Front, reversing shapings.

RIGHT MITTEN

*** With 4mm (No 8/US 6) needles and A, cast on 16 sts.

1st row and 2(3: 3) foll alt rows (wrong side) K.

2nd row [K1, m1, k6, m1, k1] twice.

4th row [K1, m1, k8, m1, k1] twice.

6th row [K1, m1, k10, m1, k1] twice.

2nd and 3rd sizes only

8th row [K1, m1, k12, m1, k1] twice.

All sizes

K 3 rows.

Next row K1, m1, k12(16: 14), [m1, k2] 1(0: 1) time, m1, k12(15: 14), [m1, k1] 1(0: 1) time. 32(34: 36) sts.

K 26(30: 34) rows.***

Change to 3¼mm (No 10/US 3) needles.

Next row Cast on 8(9: 9) sts, k0(0: 1), [p1, k1] to last 0(1: 0) st, p0(1: 0).

Next row K0(1: 0), [p1, k1] 8(8: 9) times, turn.

Work on this set of sts only. ****Rib 1 row.

1st buttonhole row Rib 3, cast off 1, rib to last 4 sts, cast off 1, rib to end.

2nd buttonhole row Rib 3, cast on 1, rib to last 3 sts, cast on 1, rib 3.

Rib 2 rows. Cast off in rib. ****

Right Sleeve

With 3¼mm (No 10/US 3) needles and right side facing, rejoin A yarn to rem sts, cast on 8(8: 9) sts, k0(0: 1), [p1, k1] to last 0(0: 1) st, p0(0: 1). 32(34: 36) sts.

***** Rib 4 rows.

Next row (wrong side) Rib 3(3: 4), m1, [rib 5(4: 3), m1] to last 4(3: 5) sts, rib to end. 38(42: 46) sts.

Change to 4mm (No 8/US 6) needles. Work in garter st, inc one st at each end of every foll 3rd(4th: 4th) row until there are 62(66: 70) sts. Cont straight until Sleeve measures 14(16: 18)cm/ 5½(6¼: 7)in from beg of rib, ending with a wrong side row. Cast off.

LEFT MITTEN

Work as given for Right Mitten from *** to ***.

Change to 3¼mm (No 10/US 3) needles.

Next row P0(1: 0), [k1, p1] 8(8: 9) times, turn.

Work on this set of sts only.

Next row [K1, p1] to last 0(1: 0) st, k0(1: 0).

Work as given for Right Mitten from **** to ****.

Left Sleeve

With 3¼mm (No 10/US 3) needles and wrong side facing, rejoin A yarn to rem sts, cast on 8(9: 9) sts, p0(1: 1), [k1, p1] to last 0(1: 0) st, k0(1: 0).

Next row Cast on 8(8: 9), p0(1: 1), [k1, p1] to last 0(1: 1) st, k0(1: 1). 32(34: 36) sts.

Complete as given for Right Sleeve from ***** to end.

NECKBAND

Join shoulder seams.

With 3¼mm (No 10/US 3) needles, right side facing and A, pick up and k19(20: 21) sts up right front neck, k back neck sts inc one st at centre, pick up and k19(20: 21) sts down left front neck. 61(63: 67) sts.

1st rib row P1, [k1, p1] to end.

2nd rib row K1, [p1, k1] to end.

Rib 4 rows more.

Next row Rib 5 and slip these 5 sts onto a safety pin, rib 5(5: 4), inc in next st, [rib 9(6: 7), inc in next st] to last 10(10: 9) sts, rib 5(5: 4), slip last 5 sts onto a safety pin. 56(60: 64) sts.

Hood

Change to 4mm (No 8/US 6) needles.

Work in garter st until Hood measures 12(14: 16)cm/4¾(5½: 6¼)in from top of rib, ending with a wrong side row.

Shape Top

Next row K37(39: 41), k2 tog, turn.

Next row K19, k2 tog tbl, turn.

Next row K19, k2 tog, turn.

Rep last 2 rows until all sts are worked off at each side of centre sts. Leave rem 20 sts on a holder.

HOOD EDGING

With 3¼mm (No 10/US 3) needles, right side facing and A, rib 5 sts from right side of hood safety pin, pick up and k26(29: 32) sts up right side of hood, k centre sts dec one st, pick up and k26(29: 32) sts down left side of hood, rib 5 sts from safety pin. 81(87: 93) sts.

Rib 7 rows. Cast off in rib.

BUTTONHOLE BAND

With 3¼mm (No 10/US 3) needles, right side facing and A, pick up and k85(93: 101) sts evenly along right side of front opening to top of hood edging. Work 3 rows in rib as given for Neckband.

1st buttonhole row Rib 3(5: 7), [cast off 1, rib 11(12: 13) sts more] 6 times, cast off 1, rib to end.

2nd buttonhole row Rib to end, casting on one st over the one cast off in previous row.

Rib 2 rows. Cast off in rib.

BUTTON BAND

Work to match Buttonhole Band omitting buttonholes.

SOLE PADS (make 2)

With 4mm (No 8/US 6) needles and B, cast on 8 sts.

Work in garter st, inc one st at each end of 2nd row and foll 4th row. 12 sts. Work 21 rows straight. Dec one st at each end of next row and foll alt row. 8 sts. K 1 row. Cast off.

PALM PADS (make 2)

With 4mm (No 8/US 6) needles and B, cast on 8 sts.

Work in garter st, inc one st at each end of 2nd row and foll 4th row. 12 sts. Work 13 rows straight. Dec one st at each end of next row and foll alt row. 8 sts. K 1 row. Cast off.

EARS (make 4)

With 4mm (No 8/US 6) needles and A, cast on 16 sts.

Work in garter st for 13 rows. Dec one st at each end of next row and 2 foll alt rows. 10 sts. K 1 row. Cast off.

EAR LININGS (make 2)

With 4mm (No 8/US 6) needles and B, cast on 12 sts.

Work in garter st for 7 rows. Dec one st at each end of next row and foll alt row. 8 sts. K 1 row. Cast off.

TO MAKE UP

Join foot and leg seams, then back crotch seam. Join front crotch and centre seam to front opening. Lap buttonhole band over button band and catch down to base of opening. Join side seams of mittens, leaving buttonhole band free. Join sleeve seams. Sew in sleeves. Sew on buttons. Join paired ear pieces together then sew ear linings in place. Sew on ears, sole and palm pads in place.

Tartan All-in-One with Patchwork Blanket and Gingham Bear

See Page
12

MATERIALS
All-in-one 5(6) 50g balls of Rowan Cotton Glace in White (A).
2 balls of same in Light Blue and 1 ball in Navy.
Pair each of 2¾mm (No 12/US 2) and 3¼mm (No 10/US 3) knitting needles.
7 buttons.
Blanket 6 50g balls of Rowan Cotton Glace in White (A).
1 ball of same in each of Light Blue and Navy.
Pair of 3¼mm (No 10/US 3) knitting needles.
Bear 1 50g ball of Rowan Cotton Glace in each of White (A), Light Blue (B) and Navy (C).
Pair of 3¼mm (No 10/US 3) knitting needles.
Stuffing.

TENSION
25 sts and 34 rows to 10cm/4in square over st st on 3¼mm (No 10/US 3) needles.
27 sts and 32 rows to 10cm/4in square over tartan or check pattern on 3¼mm (No 10/US 3) needles.

ABBREVIATIONS
See page 7.

MEASUREMENTS
All-in-one

To fit age	3-6	6-9	months
Actual chest	57	62	cm
measurement	22½	24½	in
Length	47	51	cm
	18½	20	in
Inside leg seam	14	17	cm
	5½	6¾	in
Sleeve seam	17	20	cm
	6¾	8	in

Blanket
Approximately 53cm x 72cm/21in x 28½in.
Bear
Approximately 23cm/9in high.

NOTE
Read charts from right to left on right side rows and from left to right on wrong side rows. When working in tartan pattern or colour motifs, use separate small balls of contrast yarn for each coloured area and twist yarns together on wrong side at joins to avoid holes. On tartan pattern the vertical lines in Navy can be Swiss darned (see diagram page 68) when the garment is completed. When working in check pattern, strand yarn not in use loosely across wrong side to keep fabric elastic.

All-in-one

LEFT LEG
With 2¾mm (No 12/US 2) needles and A, cast on 51(55) sts.
1st row K1, [p1, k1] to end.
This row forms moss st. Work 8 rows more.
Next row Moss st 3(4), m1, [moss st 5(4), m1] to last 3 sts, moss st 3. 61(68) sts.
Change to 3¼mm (No 10/US 3) needles.
Beg with a k row, work in st st and tartan patt from chart 1, **at the same time**, inc and work into patt one st at each end of 3rd row and 12(5) foll alt rows, then on every 3rd row until there are 93(100) sts. Patt 2(3) rows straight.
Shape Crotch
Keeping patt correct, cast off 4 sts at beg of next 2 rows. Dec one st at each end of next row and 3 foll alt rows. 77(84) sts. Work 1 row. ** Leave these sts on a spare needle.

RIGHT LEG
Work as given for Left Leg to **.

MAIN PART
Next row Patt across sts of Right Leg then Left Leg. 154(168) sts.
Cont in patt until work measures 8cm/3in from beg of crotch shaping, ending with a wrong side row.
Shape Front Opening
Next row Cast off 3, patt to end.
Next row Cast off 2, patt to end. 149(163) sts.
Cont straight until work measures 34(36)cm/13¼(14¼)in from beg, ending with a right side row.
Left Front

Next row Patt 35(39), work twice in next st, turn.
Work on this set of 37(41) sts only for a further 10(11)cm/4(4¼)in, ending with a wrong side row.
Shape Neck
Next row Patt to last 8 sts, turn; leave the 8 sts on a safety pin.
Dec one st at neck edge on every row until 24(26) sts rem. Cont straight until work measures 47(51)cm/18½(20)in from beg, ending with a wrong side row.
Shape Shoulder
Cast off 12(13) sts at beg of next row.
Work 1 row. Cast off rem 12(13) sts.
Back
With wrong side facing, rejoin yarn to rem sts, work twice in first st, patt 75(81), work twice in next st, turn.
Work on this set of 79(85) sts until work measures 47(51)cm/18½(20)in from beg, ending with a wrong side row.
Shape Shoulders
Cast off 12(13) sts at beg of next 4 rows. Leave rem 31(33) sts on a holder.
Right Front
With wrong side facing, rejoin yarn to rem sts, work twice in first st, patt to end. Complete to match Left Front, reversing shapings.

SLEEVES
With 2¾mm (No 12/US 2) needles and A, cast on 35(39) sts. Work 9 rows in moss st as given for Left Leg.
Next row Moss st 3, [m1, moss st 2] to end. 51(57) sts.
Change to 3¼mm (No 10/US 3) needles.
Beg with a k row, work in st st and tartan patt from chart 1, inc one st at each end of 3rd row and every foll 4th row until there are 71(81) sts, working inc sts into patt. Cont straight until Sleeve measures 17(20)cm/6¾(8)in from beg, ending with a wrong side row. Cast off.

BUTTONHOLE BAND
With 2¾mm (No 12/US 2) needles, right side facing and A, pick up and k55 sts along right side of front opening to neck edge. Work 3 rows in moss st as given for Left Leg.
Buttonhole row Moss st 3, [p2 tog, yrn, moss st 6] 6 times, p2 tog, yrn,

moss st 2.
Moss st 3 rows. Cast off in moss st.

BUTTON BAND
Work to match Buttonhole Band omitting buttonholes.

COLLAR
Join shoulder seams.
With 2¾mm (No 12/US 2) needles, right side facing, A and beg at centre of buttonhole band, pick up and k2 sts from band, k8 from safety pin, pick up and k16(18) sts up right front neck, k back neck sts, pick up and k16(18) sts down left front neck, k8 sts from safety pin, pick up and k2 sts to centre of button band. 83(89) sts. Work 1 row in moss st as given for Left Leg.
Next 2 rows Moss st to last 24 sts, turn.
Next 2 rows Moss st to last 20 sts, turn. Cont in this way, working 4 sts more at end of next 6 rows. Work 20 rows in moss st across all sts. Cast off loosely in moss st.

TO MAKE UP
Sew in sleeves, placing centre of sleeves to shoulders, then join sleeve seams. Join leg and crotch seams, then centre front seam. Lap buttonhole band over button band and catch down at base of opening. Sew on buttons.

Blanket

MOTIF A
Worked over 23 sts.
1st row (right side) With A, k23.
2nd row With A, p23.
3rd to 8th rows Rep 1st and 2nd rows 3 times.
9th row K6A, k11 sts of 1st row of chart 2, k6A.
10th row P6A, p11 sts of 2nd row of chart 2, p6A.
11th to 24th rows Rep 9th and 10th rows 7 times but working 3rd to 16th rows of chart.
25th to 32nd rows Rep 1st and 2nd rows 4 times.

MOTIF B
Worked in A over 23 sts.
1st row (right side) K23.
2nd row P23.
3rd to 8th rows Rep 1st and 2nd rows 3 times.
9th row K11, p1, k11.
10th row P10, k1, p1, k1, p10.
11th row K9, p1, [k1, p1] twice, k9.
12th row P8, k1, [p1, k1] 3 times, p8.
13th row K7, p1, [k1, p1] 4 times, k7.
14th row P6, k1, [p1, k1] 5 times, p6.

Key

□ = White (A)

☒ = Light Blue

◢ = Navy

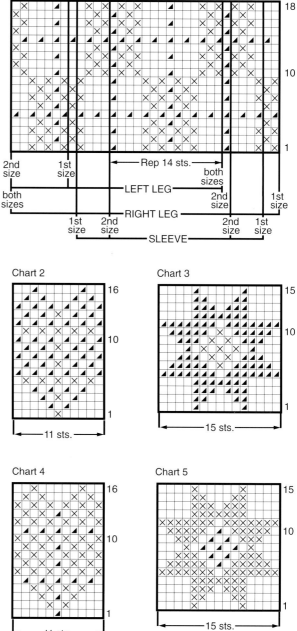

Chart 1

2nd size   1st size   ← Rep 14 sts. →   both sizes
both sizes   LEFT LEG   2nd size   1st size
RIGHT LEG
1st size   2nd size   2nd size   1st size
SLEEVE

Chart 2
11 sts.

Chart 3
15 sts.

Chart 4
11 sts.

Chart 5
15 sts.

15th to 22nd rows Rep 13th and 14th rows 4 times.
23rd row K7, p1, k1, p1, k3, p1, k1, p1, k7.
24th row P8, k1, p5, k1, p8.
25th to 32nd rows Rep 1st and 2nd rows 4 times.

MOTIF C
Worked over 23 sts.
1st row (right side) With A, k23.
2nd row With A, p23.
3rd to 8th rows Rep 1st and 2nd rows 3 times.

9th row K4A, k15 sts of 1st row of chart 3, k4A.
10th row P4A, p15 sts of 2nd row of chart 3, p4A.
11th to 23rd rows Rep 9th and 10th rows 6 times, then work 9th row again but working 3rd to 15th rows of chart.
24th row As 2nd row.
25th to 32nd rows Rep 1st and 2nd rows 4 times.

MOTIF D
Worked in A over 23 sts.
1st row (right side) K23.

2nd row P23.
3rd to 8th rows Rep 1st and 2nd rows 3 times.
9th row K8, p1, k5, p1, k8.
10th row P9, k1, p3, k1, p9.
11th row K8, p1, [k1, p1] 3 times, k8.
12th row P9, k1, [p1, k1] twice, p9.
13th row K4, p1, [k1, p1] 7 times, k4.
14th row P5, k1, [p1, k1] 6 times, p5.
15th row K6, p1, [k1, p1] 5 times, k6.
16th row P7, k1, [p1, k1] 4 times, p7.
17th row As 15th row.
18th row As 14th row.
19th row As 13th row.
20th row As 12th row.
21st row As 11th row.
22nd row As 10th row.
23rd row As 9th row.
24th row As 2nd row.
25th to 32nd rows Rep 1st and 2nd rows 4 times.

MOTIF E
Worked over 23 sts.
1st row (right side) With A, k23.
2nd row With A, p23.
3rd to 8th rows Rep 1st and 2nd rows 3 times.
9th row K6A, k11 sts of 1st row of chart 4, k6A.
10th row P6A, p11 sts of 2nd row of chart 4, p6A.
11th to 24th rows Rep 9th and 10th rows 7 times but working 3rd to 16th rows of chart.
25th to 32nd rows Rep 1st and 2nd rows 4 times.

MOTIF F
Worked over 23 sts.
1st row (right side) With A, k23.
2nd row With A, p23.
3rd to 8th rows Rep 1st and 2nd rows 3 times.
9th row K4A, k15 sts of 1st row of chart 5, k4A.
10th row P4A, p15 sts of 2nd row of chart 5, p4A.
11th to 23rd rows Rep 9th and 10th rows 6 times, then work 9th row again but working 3rd to 15th rows of chart.
24th row With A, p23.
25th to 32nd rows Rep 1st and 2nd rows 4 times.

TO MAKE
With 3¼mm (No 10/US 3) needles and A, cast on 133 sts.
1st row K1, [p1, k1] to end.
This row forms moss st. Work 3 rows more.
5th row (right side) Moss st 3, work 1st row of motif A, moss st 3, work 1st row of motif B, moss st 3, work 1st row of motif C, moss st 3, work 1st row of motif D, moss st 3, work 1st row of motif E,

moss st 3.
6th to 36th rows Work as set on last row, working 2nd to 32nd rows of motifs.
37th to 40th rows Rep 1st row 4 times.
41st row Moss st 3, work 1st row of motif D, moss st 3, work 1st row of motif E, moss st 3, work 1st row of motif B, moss st 3, work 1st row of motif F, moss st 3, work 1st row of motif D, moss st 3.
42nd to 76th rows Work 6th to 40th rows.
77th row Moss st 3, work 1st row of motif F, moss st 3, work 1st row of motif D, moss st 3, work 1st row of motif A, moss st 3, work 1 st row of motif B, moss st 3, work 1st row of motif C, moss st 3.
78th to 112th rows Work 6th to 40th rows.
113th row Moss st 3, work 1st row of motif B, moss st 3, work 1st row of motif C, moss st 3, work 1st row of motif D, moss st 3, work 1st row of motif E, moss st 3, work 1st row of motif B, moss st 3.
114th to 148th rows Work 6th to 40th rows.
149th row Moss st 3, work 1st row of motif E, moss st 3, work 1st row of motif B, moss st 3 , work 1st row of motif F, moss st 3, work 1st row of motif D, moss st 3, work 1st row of motif A, moss st 3.
150th to 184th rows Work 6th to 40th rows.
185th row Moss st 3, work 1st row of motif D, moss st 3, work 1st row of motif A, moss st 3, work 1st row of motif B, moss st 3, work 1st row of motif C, moss st 3, work 1st row of motif D, moss st 3.
186th to 220th rows Work 6th to 40th rows.
221st row Moss st 3, work 1st row of motif C, moss st 3, work 1st row of motif D, moss st 3, work 1st row of motif E, moss st 3, work 1st row of motif B, moss st 3, work 1st row of motif F, moss st 3.
222nd to 256th rows Work 6th to 40th rows.
Cast off in moss st.

Bear

LEGS (make 2)
With 3¼mm (No 10/US 3) needles and B, cast on 30 sts.
1st row (right side) K2B, [2A, 2B] to end.
2nd row P2B, [2A, 2B] to end.
3rd row K2C, [2B, 2C] to end.
4th row P2C, [2B, 2C] to end.
These 4 rows form check patt. Patt 4

rows more.
Next row Patt 9, cast off next 12 sts, patt to end.
Patt 15 rows across all sts. Cast off.

SOLES (make 2)
With 3¼mm (No 10/US 3) needles and B, cast on 12 sts.
1st row (right side) [K2B, 2A] to end.
2nd row [P2A, 2B] to end.
3rd row [K2C, 2B] to end.
4th row [P2B, 2C] to end.
Rep last 4 rows once more. Cast off.

BODY (make 2)
With 3¼mm (No 10/US 3) needles and B, cast on 22 sts. Work 26 rows in check patt as given for Legs. Cast off.

ARMS (make 2)
With 3¼mm (No 10/US 3) needles and B, cast on 18 sts. Work 22 rows in check patt as given for Legs. Cast off.

HEAD (make 2)
Work as given for Arms.

EARS (make 4)
Work as given for Soles.

TO MAKE UP
Join instep seam on legs. Rounding seam at top, join top and back leg seams, leaving an opening. Sew in soles, rounding corners. Stuff and close openings. Make darts at centre of lower and top edges of body pieces, making top darts longer. With right sides together, join body pieces together, tapering corners and leaving top edge open. Turn to right side and stuff firmly. Gather top edge, pull up and secure. Fold arms in half lengthwise, join seams tapering corners and leaving an opening. Stuff firmly and close opening. With right sides of head pieces together and leaving cast on edge free, sew around pieces, tapering corners and forming point at centre front edge for nose. Turn to right side and stuff firmly. Gather open edge, pull up and secure. Sew head in place. Attach yarn 1cm/½in down from top at centre of one arm, thread through body at shoulder position, attach other arm, then thread yarn through body in same place again, pull up tightly, attach to first arm again and fasten off. Attach legs at hip position in same way as arms. With right sides of paired ear pieces together, work seam around, tapering corners and leaving cast on edge free. Turn to right side and close opening. Sew them in place.

All-in-One with Bootees, Hat and Rabbit

See Pages
14/15

MATERIALS

All-in-one 5 50g balls of Rowan Designer DK Wool in Cream (A).
1 ball of same in each of Blue (B) and Light Brown.
Oddment of Pink and Dark Brown DK yarn.
Pair each of 3¼mm (No 10/US 3) and 4mm (No 8/US 6) knitting needles.
6 buttons.
Bootees 1 50g ball of Rowan Designer DK Wool in Light Brown (A).
Small amount of same in Pink and Cream.
Oddment of Black DK yarn.
Pair of 3¼mm (No 10/US 3) knitting needles.
Hat 1 50g ball of Rowan Designer DK Wool in Light Brown (A).
Small amount of same in Cream.
Pair of 4mm (No 8/US 6) knitting needles.
Rabbit 1 50g ball of Rowan Designer DK Wool in Light Brown (A).
1 ball of same in each of Pink and Blue.
Oddment of Dark Brown.
Pair each of 2mm (No 14/US 0) and 3¼mm (No 10/US 3) knitting needles.
Stuffing.

MEASUREMENTS

All-in-one, bootees and hat

To fit age	3-6	months
Actual chest	56	cm
measurement	22	in
Length	49	cm
	19½	in
Sleeve seam	16	cm
	6¼	in
Inside leg seam	13	cm
	5	in

Rabbit

Approximately 16cm/6¼in high.

TENSION

24 sts and 32 rows to 10cm/4in square over st st on 4mm (No 8/US 6) needles.
28 sts and 36 rows to 10cm/4in square over st st on 3¼mm (No 10/US 3) needles.

ABBREVIATIONS

See page 7.

All-in-one

LEFT LEG

With 3¼mm (No 10/US 3) needles and B, cast on 48 sts.
Change to A and work 12 rows in k1, p1 rib.
Inc row Rib 7, [m1, rib 5] to last st, rib 1. 56 sts.
Change to 4mm (No 8/US 6) needles.
Beg with a k row, work in st st, inc one st at each end of 3rd row and every foll alt row until there are 80 sts. Work 5 rows straight.
Shape Crotch
Cast off 3 sts at beg of next 2 rows.
Dec one st at each end of next row and 2 foll alt rows. 68 sts. Work 1 row. **
Leave these sts on a spare needle.

RIGHT LEG

Work as given for Left Leg to **.

MAIN PART

Next row K Right Leg sts, then Left Leg sts. 136 sts.
Cont straight for a further 7cm/2¾in, ending with a p row.
Shape Front Opening
Cast off 3 sts at beg of next 2 rows. 130 sts. Cont straight until work measures 35cm/13¾in from beg, ending with a k row.
Divide for Armholes
Next row P30, cast off 1 st, p to last 31 sts, cast off 1 st, p to end.
Right Front
Next row K30, turn.
Work on this set of sts only for 10cm/4in, ending with a p row.
Shape Neck
Next row K5 and slip these sts onto a safety pin, k to end.
Dec one st at neck edge on every row until 21 sts rem. Cont straight until work measures 49cm/19¼in from beg, ending with a k row.
Shape Shoulder
Cast off 11 sts at beg of next row. Work 1 row. Cast off rem 10 sts.

Back
With right side facing, join yarn to rem sts, k68 and turn. Cont on this set of sts only until Back matches Right Front to shoulder shaping, ending with a p row.
Shape Shoulders
Cast off 11 sts at beg of next 2 rows and 10 sts at beg of foll 2 rows. Leave rem 26 sts on a holder.
Left Front
With right side facing, rejoin yarn to rem 30 sts and complete to match Right Front, reversing shapings.

SLEEVES

With 3¼mm (No 10/US 3) needles and B, cast on 40 sts.
Change to A and work 10 rows in k1, p1 rib, inc 4 sts evenly across last row. 44 sts.
Change to 4mm (No 8/US 6) needles.
Beg with a k row, work in st st, inc one st at each end of every 3rd row until there are 68 sts. Cont straight until Sleeve measures 16cm/6¼in from beg, ending with a p row. Cast off.

NECKBAND

Join shoulder seams.
With 3¼mm (No 10/US 3) needles and right side facing, slip 5 sts from right front safety pin onto needle, join in A yarn and pick up and k18 sts up right front neck, k back neck sts dec one st, pick up and k18 sts down left front neck, k5 sts from safety pin. 71 sts.
1st rib row K1, [p1, k1] to end.
2nd rib row P1, [k1, p1] to end.
Rib 3 rows more. Change to B and cast off in rib.

BUTTONHOLE BAND

With 3¼mm (No 10/US 3) needles and A, pick up and k57 sts along right edge of front opening to top of neckband.
Work 3 rows in rib as given for Neckband.
Buttonhole row Rib 3, [yrn, p2 tog, rib 8] 5 times, yrn, p2 tog, rib 2.
Rib 3 rows. Change to B and cast off in rib to last st, then pick up and cast off 6 sts along row end edge of band.
Fasten off.

BUTTON BAND

Work to match Buttonhole Band omitting buttonholes.

(see diagram page 68)
... motif (see chart on page 46) on
...eft front. With Dark Brown, embroider
eyes, nose and mouth on rabbit. Sew in
sleeves, placing centre of sleeves to
shoulder seams. Join sleeve seams.
Join leg and crotch seams, then centre
front seam to opening. Lap buttonhole
band over button band and catch down
at base of opening. Sew on buttons.

Bootees

MAIN PART

With 3¼mm (No 10/US 3) needles and
A, cast on 36 sts. K 5 rows. Beg with a
k row, work 7 rows in st st. K 2 rows.
Work 10 rows in k1, p1 rib inc 3 sts
evenly across last row. 39 sts.
Beg with a k row, work 4 rows in st st.

Shape Instep

Next row K26, turn.
Next row P13, turn.
Work 13 rows in st st on these 13 sts
only.
Next row: P3, [p2 tog, p3] twice.
Break off yarn.
With right side facing, rejoin yarn at
base of instep, pick up and k8 sts
along side edge of instep, k11 sts of
instep, pick up and k8 sts along other
side of instep, k rem 13 sts. 53 sts. Beg
with a p row, work 14 rows in st st.
Next row [P next st tog with
corresponding st 7 rows below] to end.

Shape Sole

Next row Sl first 21 sts onto right hand
needle, rejoin yarn and k10, k2 tog,
turn.
Next row Sl 1, k9, k2 tog tbl, turn.
Next row Sl 1, k9, k2 tog, turn.
Rep last 2 rows 8 times more, then work
first of the 2 rows again.
Next row Sl 1, k3, sl 1, k2 tog, psso, k3,
k2 tog, turn.
Next row Sl 1, k7, k2 tog tbl, turn.
Next row Sl 1, k7, k2 tog, turn.
Rep last 2 rows once more, then work
first of the 2 rows again.
Next row Sl 1, k2, sl 1, k2 tog, psso, k2,
k2 tog, turn.
Next row Sl 1, k5, k2 tog tbl, turn.
Next row Sl 1, k5, k2 tog, turn.
Rep last 2 rows 3 times more.
Next row Sl 1, k2, k2 tog, k1, k2 tog tbl.
Place rem 3 sts at each side of sole on
one needle, pointing in same direction
as needle with sole sts. With right sides
together, cast off tog rem sts.

OUTER EARS (make 2)

With 3¼mm (No 10/US 3) needles and
A, cast on 7 sts. Beg with a k row, work
16 rows in st st.
Next row K1, [k2 tog, k1] twice.
Work 3 rows.
Next row K2 tog, k1, k2 tog.
Work 3 rows. Work 3 tog. Fasten off.

INNER EARS (make 2)

With 3¼mm (No 10/US 3) needles and
Pink, cast on 5 sts. Beg with a k row,
work 16 rows in st st.
Next row K2 tog, k1, k2 tog.
Work 3 rows. Work 3 tog. Fasten off.

NOSE

With 3¼mm (No 10/US 3) needles and
Black, cast on 1st.
Next row [K1, p1, k1, p1, k1] in st.
Next row K to end, then pass 2nd,
3rd, 4th and 5th st over first st.
Fasten off.

TO MAKE UP

Join back seam of main part, reversing
seam on cuff. Turn back cuff. Sew
inner ears to outer ears. Fold in half at
cast on edge and stitch together first 4
rows of outer layers. Sew ears in
place. Form nose into a ball and sew in
place. With Cream, make a small pom-
pom and attach to back of bootee.
Make one more.

Hat

With 4mm (No 8/US 6) needles and A,
cast on 91 sts.
1st rib row K1, [p1, k1] to end.
2nd rib row P1, [k1, p1] to end.
Beg with a k row, work 7 rows in st st.
Beg with a k row (thus reversing
fabric), work in st st until Hat measures
16cm/6¼in from beg, ending with a p
row.
Next row [K8, k2 tog] to last st, k1.
Work 3 rows.
Next row [K7, k2 tog] to last st, k1.
Work 3 rows.
Next row [K6, k2 tog] to last st, k1.
Cont in this way, dec 9 sts as set on
every 4th row until 19 sts rem. P 1 row.
Next row [K2 tog] to last st, k1.
Break off yarn, thread end through rem
sts, pull up and secure. Join seam,
reversing seam on brim. Turn back
brim. With Cream, make a pon-pom
and attach to top of Hat.

Rabbit

LEGS (make 2)

With 3¼mm (No 10/US 3) needles and
A, cast on 12 sts.
P 1 row.
Next row K1, [m1, k1] to end.
P 1 row.
Next row K1, m1, k8, [m1, k1] 6 times,
k7, m1, k1. 31 sts.
Work 3 rows in st st.
Next row K13, k2 tog, k1, skpo, k13.
P1 row.
Next row K12, k2 tog, k1, skpo, k12. 27
sts.
P 1 row.
Next row K7, cast off next 13 sts, k to end.
Work 9 rows across all sts, inc one st at
each end of 2nd row. 16 sts.
Next row [K1, skpo, k3, k2 tog] twice.
P 1 row.
Next row [K1, skpo, k1, k2 tog] twice.
Next row [P2 tog] to end.
Break off yarn, thread end through rem
sts, pull up and secure. Join instep,
sole and back leg seam, leaving an
opening. Stuff and close opening.

BODY

Begin at neck edge.
With 3¼mm (No 10/US 3) needles and
A, cast on 15 sts.
P 1 row.
Next row K1, [m1, k1] to end. 29 sts.
Beg with a p row, work 5 rows in st st.
Next row [K7, m1] twice, k1, [m1, k7]
twice.
Work 3 rows.
Next row K16, m1, k1, m1, k16. 35 sts.
Work 5 rows.
Next row K15, skpo, k1, k2 tog, k15.
Work 3 rows.
Next row K14, skpo, k1, k2 tog, k14.
Work 3 rows.
Next row K1, [k2 tog] to end. 16 sts.
P 1 row. Cast off.

ARMS (make 2)

With 3¼mm (No 10/US 3) needles and A,
cast on 6 sts.
P 1 row.
Next row K1, [m1, k1] to end.
P 1 row.
Next row K1, [m1, k4, m1, k1] twice. 15
sts.
Work 7 rows.
Next row K1, [skpo, k2, k2 tog, k1] twice.
Work 13 rows, inc one st at each end of
4th row. 13 sts.
Next row K1, [skpo, k1, k2 tog, k1] twice.
P 1 row.
Next row K1, [k2 tog] to end. 5 sts.
Break off yarn, thread end through rem
sts, pull up and secure. Join underarm
seam, leaving an opening. Stuff and
close opening.

HEAD

Begin at back.
With 3¼mm (No 10/US 3) needles and A, cast on 7 sts.
P 1 row.
Next row K1, [m1, k1] to end.
Rep last 2 rows once more. 25 sts.
Work 3 rows in st st.
Next row K1, [m1, k3] to end. 33 sts.
Work 13 rows.
Next row K1, [k2 tog] to end.
Work 5 rows.
Next row K1, [k2 tog] to end. 9 sts.
P 1 row. Break off yarn, thread end through rem sts, pull up and secure. Join seam, leaving an opening. Stuff and close opening.

OUTER EARS (make 2)

With 3¼mm (No 10/US 3) needles and A, cast on 4 sts.
K 1 row.
Next row K1, [m1, k1] to end.
K 1 row.
Next row K3, m1, k1, m1, k3. 9 sts.
K 30 rows.
Next row Skpo, k to last 2 sts, k2 tog.
K 1 row. Rep last 2 rows twice more. K 1 row. K3 tog and fasten off.

INNER EARS (make 2)

With 2mm (No 14/US 0) needles and Pink, work as given for Outer Ears.

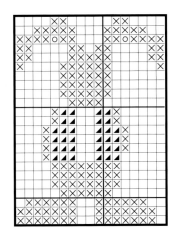

Key

▤ = Blue (B)

☒ = Light Brown

◉ = Pink

WAISTCOAT

With 3¼mm (No 10/US 3) needles and Blue, cast on 24 sts for back.
K 14 rows. Cast off 6 sts at beg of next 2 rows. 12 sts. K 10 rows.
Next row K4, turn.

Work on this set of sts only for right front. K 4 rows.
Next row K1, m1, k to end.
K 3 rows.
Next row K1, m1, k to end.
K 2 rows.
Cast on 6 st at beg of next row. 12 sts.
K 15 rows. Cast off.
Rejoin yarn at neck edge to rem sts, cast off 4 sts, k to end. K 4 rows.
Next row K to last st, m1, k1.
K 3 rows. Rep last 4 rows once more.
Cast on 6 sts at beg of next row. 12 sts.
K14 rows. Cast off. Join side seams.

TO MAKE UP

Fold sides of body to centre, then join cast off edge. Gather neck edge, pull up and secure. Join back seam, leaving an opening. Stuff and close opening. Sew inner ears to outer ears. Fold cast on edges in half and catch stitch outside edges. Sew head in position, then sew on ears. With Dark Brown, embroider nose, mouth and eyes. Attach yarn at seam about 1cm/¼in below top of one arm, thread yarn through body at shoulder position, then attach other arm, pull yarn tightly and thread through body again in same place, then attach yarn to first arm again and fasten off. Attach legs at hip position in same way as arms.

Smock with Sheep and Shoes

See Pages 8/9, 13, & 16/17

MATERIALS

Smock 7(8) 50g balls of Rowan Cotton Glace.
Pair of 3¼mm (No 10/US 3) knitting needles.
Cable needle.
6 buttons.
Shoes 1 50g ball of Rowan Cotton Glace.
Pair of 3mm (No 11/US 2) knitting needles.
Cable needle.
2 buttons.
Sheep Small amount of Rowan Designer DK Wool in each of Cream (A) and Black (B).
Pair of 3¼mm (No 10/US 3) knitting needles.
Small amount of stuffing.

TENSION

25 sts and 34 rows to 10cm/4in square over st st on 3¼mm (No 10/US 3) needles using Cotton Glace yarn.

MEASUREMENTS

To fit age	6	12	months
Actual chest	52	57	cm
measurement	20½	22½	in
Length	36	40	cm
	14¼	15¾	in
Sleeve seam	18	20	cm
	7	8	in

ABBREVIATIONS

C2B = sl next st onto cable needle and leave at back of work, k1, then k1 from cable needle;
C2F = sl next st onto cable needle and leave at front of work, k1, then k1 from cable needle;
Cr2L = sl next st onto cable needle and leave at front of work, p1, then k1 from cable needle;
Cr2R = sl next st onto cable needle and leave at back of work, k1, then p1 from cable needle.
Also see page 7.

Smock

BACK

With 3¼mm (No 10/US 3) needles cast on 105(115) sts.
1st row K1, [p1, k1] to end.
This row forms moss st. Rep last row 5 times more.
Beg with a k row, work in st st until Back measures 23(26)cm/9(10¼)in from beg, ending with a k row.
Dec row P2(3), [p2 tog, p2, p2 tog, p3] 11(12) times, p2 tog, p2. 82(90) sts.
Work in yoke patt as follows:
1st row (right side) P4, [C2F, p6] to last 6 sts, C2F, p4.
2nd row K3, [Cr2L, Cr2R, k4] to last 7 sts, Cr2L, Cr2R, k3.
3rd row P2, [Cr2R, p2, Cr2L, p2] to end.
4th row K1, [Cr2L, k4, Cr2R] to last st, k1.
5th row P1, k1, [p6, C2B] to last 8 sts, p6, k1, p1.
6th row K1, [Cr2R, k4, Cr2L] to last st, k1.
7th row P2, [Cr2L, p2, Cr2R, p2] to end.
8th row K3, [Cr2R, Cr2L, k4] to last 7 sts, Cr2R, Cr2L, k3.
These 8 rows form yoke patt. Cont in yoke patt until Back measures 36(40)cm/14¼(15¾)in from beg, ending with a right side row.
Shape Neck and Shoulder
Next row Patt 30(33), cast off next 22(24) sts, patt to end.
Work on last set of sts only. Cast off 8(9) sts at beg of next row and 3 sts at beg of foll row. Rep last 2 rows once more. Cast off rem 8(9) sts.
With right side facing, rejoin yarn to rem sts and patt to end. Complete as given for first side.

LEFT FRONT

With 3¼mm (No 10/US 3) needles cast on 59(65) sts. Work 6 rows in moss st as given for Back.
Next row (right side) K to last 4 sts, moss st 4.
Next row Moss st 4, p to end.
Rep last 2 rows until Front measures 23(26)cm/9(10¼)in from beg, ending with a right side row.
Dec row Moss st 4, [p2 tog, p2] to last 3(9) sts, [p2 tog, p1] 1(3) times. 45(49) sts.
Work in yoke patt as follows:
1st row P4, [C2F, p6] to last 9(13) sts, C2F, p3(6), k0(1), moss st 4.
2nd row Moss st 4, [Cr2R] 0(1) time, k2(4), [Cr2L, Cr2R, k4] to last 7 sts,

Cr2L, Cr2R, k3.
3rd row P2, [Cr2R, p2, Cr2L, p2] to last 11(7) sts, Cr2R, p2(1), [Cr2L, p1] 1(0) time, moss st 4.
4th row Moss st 4, [k2, Cr2R] 0(1) times, [Cr2L, k4, Cr2R] to last st, k1.
5th row P1, k1, [p6, C2B] to last 11(7) sts, p6(3), k1(0), moss st 4.
6th row Moss st 4, [k2, Cr2L] 0(1) time, [Cr2R, k4, Cr2L] to last st, k1.
7th row P2, [Cr2L, p2, Cr2R, p2] to last 11(7) sts, Cr2L, p2(1), [Cr2R, p1] 1(0) time, moss st 4.
8th row Moss st 4, [Cr2L] 0(1) time, k2(4), [Cr2R, Cr2L, k4] to last 7 sts, Cr2R, Cr2L, k3.
These 8 rows form yoke patt. Cont in yoke patt until Front measures 33(37)cm/13(14½)in from beg, ending with a right side row.
Shape Neck
Keeping patt correct, cast off 11(12) sts at beg of next row and 4 sts at beg of 2 foll alt rows. Dec one st at neck edge on next 2 rows. 24(27) sts. Cont straight for a few rows until Front matches Back to shoulder shaping, ending with a wrong side row.
Shape Shoulder
Cast off 8(9) sts at beg of next row and foll alt row. Work 1 row. Cast off rem 8(9) sts.
Mark front edge to indicate position of 6 buttons: first one 16cm/6¼in from lower edge, last one 1cm/¼in down from neck edge and rem 4 evenly spaced between.

RIGHT FRONT

With 3¼mm (No 10/US 3) needles cast on 59(65) sts. Work 6 rows in moss st as given for Back.
Next row (right side) Moss st 4, k to end.
Next row P to last 4 sts, moss st 4.
Rep last 2 rows until Front measures 16cm/6¼in from beg, ending with a wrong side row.
Buttonhole row (right side) K1, p1, yrn, p2 tog, patt to end.
Cont until Front measures 23(26)cm/9(10¼)in from beg, ending with a right side row and making buttonholes to match markers on Left Front.
Dec row [P1, p2 tog] 1(3) times, [p2, p2 tog] to last 4 sts, moss st 4. 45(49) sts.
Work in yoke patt as follows:
1st row Moss st 4, k0(1), p3(6), C2F, [p6, C2F] to last 4 sts, p4.

2nd row K3, Cr2L, Cr2R, [k4, Cr2L, Cr2R] to last 6(10) sts, k2(4), [Cr2L] 0(1) time, moss st 4.
These 2 rows set position of yoke patt. Complete to match Left Front, making buttonholes at markers as before and reversing shapings.

SLEEVES

With 3¼mm (No 10/US 3) needles cast on 34(42) sts. Work 9 rows in yoke patt as given for Back.
Inc row P3, m1, *p4, m1, [p2, m1] twice; rep from * to last 7 sts, p4, m1, [p2, m1] 1(0) time, p1(3). 46(56) sts.
Beg with a k row, work in st st, inc one st at each end of 2nd row and every foll 3rd row until there are 70(78) sts. Work 1(8) rows straight.
Next row K18, work 1st row of yoke patt as given for Back across next 34(42) sts, k18.
Next row P18, work 2nd row of yoke patt, p18.
Work a further 15 rows as set. Cast off.

COLLAR

With 3¼mm (No 10/US 3) needles cast on 59(67) sts. Work 6 rows in moss st patt as given for Back.
1st row (right side) Moss st 2, p4, C2F, p4, k35(43), p4, C2F, p4, moss st 2.
2nd row Moss st 2, k3, Cr2L, Cr2R, k3, p35(43), k3, Cr2L, Cr2R, k3, moss st 2.
3rd row Moss st 2, p2, Cr2R, p2, Cr2L, p2, k35(43), p2, Cr2R, p2, Cr2L, p2, moss st 2.
4th row Moss st 2, k1, Cr2L, k4, Cr2R, k1, p35(43), k1, Cr2L, k4, Cr2R, k1, moss st 2.
5th row Moss st 2, p1, k1, p6, k1, p1, k35(43), p1, k1, p6, k1, p1, moss st 2.
6th row Moss st 2, k1, Cr2R, k4, Cr2L, k1, p35(43), k1, Cr2R, k4, Cr2L, k1, moss st 2.
7th row Moss st 2, p2, Cr2L, p2, Cr2R, p2, k35(43), p2, Cr2L, p2, Cr2R, p2, moss st 2.
8th row Moss st 2, k3, Cr2R, Cr2L, k3, p35(43), k3, Cr2R, Cr2L, k3, moss st 2.
These 8 rows form patt. Patt 19(23) rows more.
Shape Neck
Next row Patt 20(23), cast off next 19(21) sts, patt to end.
Work on last set of sts only for right side of front collar. Dec one st at inside edge on next 4 rows. 16(19) sts. Patt 8 rows. Inc one st at inside edge on next 6 rows. Patt 1 row.
Next row Cast on 7(8) sts, k1, p1, patt to end. 29(33) sts.
Next row Patt to last 2 sts, p1, k1.
Work a further 16(20) rows. Moss st 6 rows across all sts. Cast off in moss st. With right side facing, rejoin yarn to

rem sts and complete left side of front collar to match right side.

POCKETS (make 2)

With 3¼mm (No 10/US 3) needles cast on 19(23) sts. Beg with a k row, work 4 rows in st st.
1st row (right side) K9(11), p1, k9(11).
2nd row P8(10), k1, p1, k1, p8(10).
3rd row K7(9), p1, [k1, p1] twice, k7(9).
4th row P6(8), k1, [p1, k1] 3 times, p6(8).
5th row K5(7), p1, [k1, p1] 4 times, k5(7).
6th and 7th rows As 4th and 5th rows.
8th row P4(6), k1, [p1, k1] 5 times, p4(6).
9th row As 5th row.
10th and 11th rows As 8th and 9th rows.
12th row As 8th row.
13th row K5(7), p1, k1, p1, k3, p1, k1, p1, k5(7).
14th row P6(8), k1, p5, k1, p6(8).
Beg with a k row, work 4 rows in st st. Work 4 rows in moss st as given for Back. Cast off in moss st.

TO MAKE UP

Join shoulder seams. Sew on sleeves, placing centre of sleeves to shoulder seams. Join side and sleeve seams. Sew on pockets and buttons. Sew collar in place.

Shoes

LEFT SHOE

With 3mm (No 11/US 2) needles cast on 34(40) sts. K 1 row.
1st row K1, yf, k15(18), yf, [k1, yf] twice, k15(18), yf, k1.
2nd row and every foll alt row K to end, working tbl into each yf of previous row.
3rd row K2, yf, k15(18), yf, k2, yf, k3, yf, k15(18), yf, k2.
5th row K3, yf, k15(18), yf, [k4, yf] twice, k15(18), yf, k3.
7th row K4, yf, k15(18), yf, k5, yf, k6, yf, k15(18), yf, k4.
9th row K5, yf, k15(18), yf, [k7, yf] twice, k15(18), yf, k5.
11th row K2, [yf, k4] 7 times, [yf, k3] 0(2) times, [yf, k4] 7 times, yf, k1. 74(82) sts.
12th row Working tbl into each yf of previous row, work as follows: k4, [p2, k6] to last 6 sts, p2, k4.
Work 9 rows of yoke patt as given for Back of Smock.
Next row K4, [p2 tog, k6] to last 6 sts, p2 tog, k4. 65(72) sts.
Next row K38(42), skpo, turn.

Next row Sl 1, p11(12), p2 tog, turn.
Next row Sl 1, k11(12), skpo, turn.
Rep last 2 rows 6(7) times more, then work first of the 2 rows again.
Next row Sl 1, k to end.
Cast off knitwise, dec one st in each corner. Join back and sole seam. With 3mm (No 11/US 2) needles, right side facing and beg and ending within 8 sts of back seam, pick up and k17 sts along back heel. K 1 row. **
Next row Cast on 19, k to end, turn and cast on 3 sts.
K 1 row.
Buttonhole row K2, yf, k2 tog, k to end.
K 2 rows. Cast off. Sew on button.

RIGHT SHOE

Work as given for Left Shoe to **.
Next row Cast on 3, k to end, turn and cast on 19 sts.
K 1 row.
Buttonhole row K to last 4 sts, skpo, yf, k2.
K 2 rows. Cast off. Sew on button.

Sheep

BODY AND HEAD

With 3¼mm (No 10/US 3) needles and A, cast on 20 sts. K 16 rows.
Next row K2 tog, k to last 2 sts, k2 tog.
K 1 row.
Rep last 2 rows twice more.
Change to B. Beg with a k row, work 8 rows in st st. Break off yarn, thread end through sts, pull up and secure.

LEGS (make 4)

With 3¼mm (No 10/US 3) needles and B, cast on 7 sts. Work 7 rows in st st. Break off yarn, thread end through sts, pull up and secure.

EARS (make 2)

With 3¼mm (No 10/US 3) needles and B, cast on 5 sts. K 2 rows.
Next row K2 tog, k1, k2 tog .
K 1 row. K 3 tog and fasten off.

TAIL

With 3¼mm (No 10/US 3) needles and B, cast on 4 sts. Work 4 rows in st st. Cast off.

TO MAKE UP

Fold body in half lengthwise and join underside seam, leaving cast on edge free. Stuff lightly and close opening. Fold legs and tail in half lengthwise and join seams. Sew legs, tail and ears in place. With A, embroider eyes.

Bunny and Chick Jacket

See Pages
20 & 38

MATERIALS
4 50g balls of Rowan Designer DK
Wool in Cream (A).
2 balls of same in Pale Blue.
1 ball of same in each of Yellow (B),
Purple, Green and Brown.
Pair each of 3¼mm (No 10/US 3) and
4mm (No 8/US 6) knitting needles.
One 3¼mm (No 10/US 3) circular
knitting needle.
6 buttons.

MEASUREMENTS

To fit age	3-4	years
Actual chest	81	cm
measurement	32	in
Length	41	cm
	16¼	in
Sleeve seam	21	cm
	8¼	in

TENSION
24 sts and 32 rows to 10cm/4in square
over st st on 4mm (No 8/US 6)
needles.

ABBREVIATIONS
See page 7.

NOTE
Read charts from right to left on right
side (k) rows and from left to right on
wrong side (p) rows. When working
motifs of pattern, use separate lengths
of contrast colour for each coloured
area and twist yarns together on
wrong sides at joins to avoid holes.
Strand yarn not in use loosely across
wrong side over no more than 5 sts at
the time when working Fair Isle bands
of pattern to keep fabric elastic.

BACK
With 3¼mm (No 10/US 3) needles and
B, cast on 98 sts.
Beg with a k row, work 4 rows in st st.
Change to A.
1st rib row (right side) K2, [p2, k2] to
end.
2nd rib row P2, [k2, p2] to end.
Rib a further 10 rows.
Change to 4mm (No 8/US 6) needles.
Beg with a k row, work in st st and patt
from chart 1 until 72nd row of chart 1
has been worked, then work 1st to 40th
row of chart 2.
Shape Shoulders
With A, cast off 15 sts at beg of next 2

rows and 16 sts at beg of foll 2 rows.
Leave rem 36 sts on a holder.

LEFT FRONT
With 3¼mm (No 10/US 3) needles and
B, cast on 51 sts.
Beg with a k row, work 4 rows in st st.
Change to A.
1st rib row (right side) [K2, p2] to last
3 sts, k3.
2nd rib row P3, [k2, p2] to end.
Rib a further 10 rows, dec one st at
centre of last row. 50 sts.
Change to 4mm (No 8/US 6) needles.
Beg with a k row, work in st st and patt
from chart 1 until 72nd row of chart 1

Chart 1

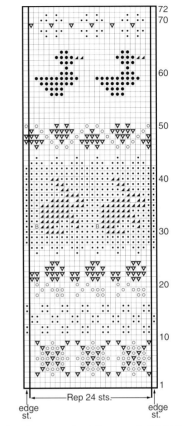

has been worked, then work 1st to 8th
rows of chart 2.
Shape Neck
Cont working from chart 2, dec one st
at neck edge on next 10 rows, then on
every alt row until 31 sts rem. Patt 4
rows.

Chart 2

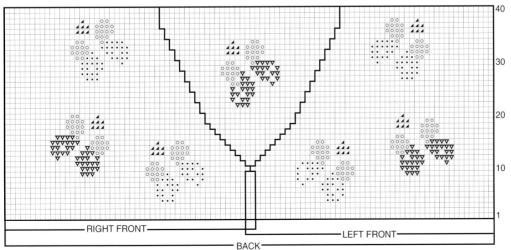

Key

☐ = Cream (A)

• = Yellow (B)

▽ = Purple

◉ = Green

⊡ = Pale Blue

◣ = Brown

B = with A, [k1, p1, k1, p1, k1]
all in next st, then pass
2nd, 3rd, 4th and 5th
st over first st.

Shape Shoulder
With A, cast off 15 sts at beg of next row. Work 1 row. Cast off rem 16 sts.

RIGHT FRONT

With 3¼mm (No 10/US 3) needles and B, cast on 51 sts.
Beg with a k row, work 4 rows in st st. Change to A.
1st rib row (right side) K3, [p2, k2] to end.
2nd rib row [P2, k2] to last 3 sts, p3.
Complete to match Left Front, reversing shoulder shaping.

SLEEVES

With 3¼mm (No 10/US 3) needles and B, cast on 50 sts.
Beg with a k row, work 4 rows in st st. Change to A and rib 12 rows as given for Back.
Change to 4mm (No 8/US 6) needles. Beg with a k row, work in st st and patt from chart 1, inc one st at each end of 7 foll 3rd rows, then on 6 foll 4th rows, working inc sts into patt. 76 sts. Patt 7 rows straight. Cast off.

FRONT BAND

Join shoulder seams.
With 3¼mm (No 10/US 3) circular needle, A, right side facing and beg on 1st row of rib, pick up and k75 sts along straight right front edge to beg of neck shaping, 34 sts up shaped edge to shoulder, k back neck sts, pick up and k34 sts down shaped left front edge to beg of neck shaping, then 75 sts along straight edge, ending on 1st row of rib. 254 sts. Work backwards and forwards. Beg with a 2nd row, work 2 rows in rib as given for Back.
1st buttonhole row Rib to last 74 sts, [cast off 2, rib 11 sts more] 5 times, cast off 2, rib to end.
2nd buttonhole row Rib to end, casting on 2 sts over those cast off in previous row.
Rib 1 row. Change to B. Beg with a k row, work 4 rows in st st. Cast off.

TO MAKE UP

Sew on sleeves, placing centre of sleeves to shoulder seams. Join side and sleeve seams, reversing seams on st st sections at lower edges. With Brown, embroider feet, legs and eyes on each chick and body of each butterfly and its antenna.

Nursery Cardigan

See Page
18

MATERIALS

5 50g balls of Rowan DK Handknit Cotton in Cream (A).
1 ball of same in each of Red, Blue, Purple, Green, Gold, Brown and Navy.
Pair of 4mm (No 8/US 6) knitting needles.
Medium size crochet hook.
5 buttons.

MEASUREMENTS

To fit age	9-12	months
Actual chest	66	cm
measurement	26	in
Length	31	cm
	12¼	in
Sleeve seam	18	cm
	7	in

TENSION

20 sts and 28 rows to 10cm/4in square over st st on 4mm (No 8/US 6) needles.

ABBREVIATIONS

Ch = chain; dc = double crochet; ss = slip stitch; tr = treble.
Also see page 7.

NOTE

Read chart from right to left on right side (k) rows and from left to right on wrong side (p) rows. When working in pattern, use separate lengths of contrast colours for each coloured area and twist yarns together on wrong side at joins to avoid holes.

BACK

With 4mm (No 8/US 6) needles and A, cast on 66 sts.
Beg with a k row, work in st st and patt from chart until 84th row of chart has been worked.
Shape Shoulders
With A, cast off 11 sts at beg of next 4 rows. Cast off rem 22 sts.

LEFT FRONT

With 4mm (No 8/US 6) needles and A, cast on 32 sts.
Beg with a k row, work in st st and patt from chart until 60th row of chart has been worked.
Shape Neck
Cont working from chart, dec one st at neck edge on next row and every foll alt row until 22 sts rem. Cont straight until 84th row of chart has been worked.
Shape Shoulder
With A, cast off 11 sts at beg of next row. Work 1 row. Cast off rem 11 sts.

RIGHT FRONT

Work as given for Left Front, working 1 row more in A before shoulder shaping.

SLEEVES

With 4mm (No 8/US 6) needles and A, cast on 34 sts.
Beg with a k row, work 3 rows in st st. Beg with 15th row, work in patt from chart, **at the same time**, inc one st at each end of 2nd row and every foll 4th row until there are 54 sts. Patt 7 rows. Cast off.

TO MAKE UP

Join shoulder seams. Sew on sleeves, placing centre of sleeves to shoulder seams. Join side and sleeve seams.
Crochet edging With crochet hook, A, right side facing and beg at Right Front side seam, work 1 round of dc (the number of dc should be divisible by 3) along cast on edge then front edge of Right Front working 3 dc in corner, across back neck, down front edge and cast on edge of Left Front working 3 dc in corner, then cast on edge of Back, ss in first dc.
Next round [2 tr in same dc as ss, miss 2 dc, ss in next dc] to end, making 5 buttonholes along straight edge of Right Front by working 3 ch, miss 2 dc, ss in next dc. Fasten off.
Work crochet edging along cast on edge of sleeves. Sew on buttons. With Navy, embroider eye on rocking horses.

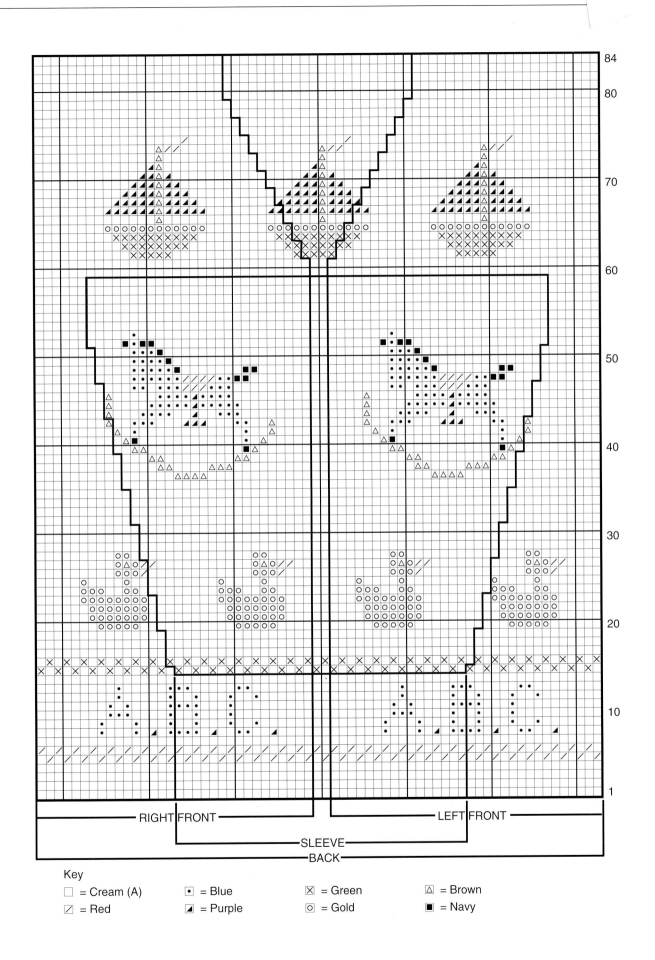

84
80
70
60
50
40
30
20
10
1

RIGHT FRONT

LEFT FRONT

SLEEVE

BACK

Key

☐ = Cream (A)   · = Blue   ⊠ = Green   △ = Brown

╱ = Red   ◢ = Purple   ⊙ = Gold   ■ = Navy

Fair Isle Ballet Top with Shoes and Teddy with Dress

See Pages

13 & 21

MATERIALS

Top 2 50g balls of Rowan True 4 ply Botany in Cream (A).
1 ball of same in each of Yellow, Red, Green and Navy.
Pair each of 2¾mm (No 12/US 2) and 3¼ mm (No 10/US 3) knitting needles.
Shoes Small amount of Rowan True 4 ply Botany in each of Cream (A), Yellow, Red, Green and Navy.
Pair of 2¾mm (No 12/US 2) knitting needles.
2 buttons.
Teddy 1 50g ball of Rowan Designer DK Wool in Brown (A).
1 50g ball of Rowan True 4 ply Botany in Red (B).
Small amount of 4 ply yarn in Navy (C).
Oddment of Black for embroidery.
Pair each of 2¾mm (No 12/US 2) and 3¼mm (No 10/US 3) knitting needles.
Stuffing.

TENSION

30 sts and 34 rows to 10cm/4in square over pattern on 3¼mm (No 10/US 3) needles using 4 ply yarn.
28 sts and 36 rows to 10cm/4in square over st st on 3¼mm (No 10/US 3) needles using DK yarn.

MEASUREMENTS

Top and Shoes

To fit age	3-6	6-9	months
Top			
Actual chest	52	56	cm
measurement	20½	22	in
Length	22	25	cm
	8½	10	in
Sleeve seam	15	17	cm
	6	6¾	in

Teddy
Approximately 18cm/7in high.

ABBREVIATIONS

See page 7.

NOTE

Read charts from right to left on right side (k) rows and from left to right on wrong side (p) rows. When working in pattern, strand yarn not in use loosely across wrong side over no more than 5 sts at the time to keep fabric elastic.

Top

BACK

With 2¾mm (No 12/US 2) needles and A, cast on 79(85) sts.
1st rib row (right side) K1, [p1, k1] to end.
2nd rib row P1, [k1, p1] to end. **
Rep last 2 rows 3 times more.
Change to 3¼mm (No 10/US 3) needles.
Beg with a k row, work in st st and patt from chart 1 until Back measures 11(13)cm/4¼(5¼)in from beg, ending with a wrong side row.
Shape Armholes
Keeping patt correct, cast off 4 sts at beg of next 2 rows. Dec one st at each end of next 4 rows. 63(69) sts. Cont straight until Back measures 22(25)cm/8½(10)in from beg, ending with a wrong side row.
Shape Shoulders
Cast off 8(9) sts at beg of next 2 rows and 9 sts at beg of foll 2 rows. Cast off rem 29(33) sts.

LEFT FRONT

Work as given for Back to **. Rib 5 rows more.
Next row Cast off 6 sts, rib to end. 73(79) sts.
Change to 3¼mm (No 10/US 3) needles.
Beg with a k row, work 2 rows in st st and patt from chart 1.
Shape Front
Keeping patt correct, dec one st at end of next row and at same edge on foll 2 rows, then work 1 row straight.
Rep last 4 rows until Front measures same as Back to armhole shaping, ending with a wrong side row.
Shape Armhole
Cont to dec at front edge as before, **at the same row**, cast off 4 sts at beg of next row, then dec one st at armhole edge on foll 4 rows. Keeping armhole edge straight, cont to dec at front edge until 17(18) sts rem. Cont straight until Front measures same as Back to shoulder shaping, ending with a wrong side row.

Shape Shoulder
Cast off 8(9) sts at beg of next row.
Work 1 row. Cast off rem 9 sts.

RIGHT FRONT

Work as given for Back to **. Rib 5 rows more.
Next row Rib to end, turn and cast off first 6 sts. 73(79) sts.
Change to 3¼mm (No 10/US 3) needles.
Complete as given for Left Front, reversing all shapings.

SLEEVES

With 2¾mm (No 12/US 2) needles and A, cast on 31(35) sts.
Work 15 rows in rib as given for Back.
Inc row [Rib 1, inc in next st, rib 2, inc in next st] 6 times, rib 1, [inc in next st, rib 1] 0(2) times. 43(49) sts.
Change to 3¼mm (No 10/US 3) needles.
Beg with a k row and 45th row of chart 1, work in st st and patt from chart 1 as indicated for Back, **at the same time,** inc one st at each end of 3rd row and every foll 4th row until there are 59(65) sts, working inc sts into patt. Cont straight until Sleeve measures approximately 15(17)cm/6(6¾)in from beg, ending with same patt row as Back before armhole shaping.
Shape Top
Cast off 4 sts at beg of next 2 rows.
Dec one st at each end of next row and 3(4) foll alt rows, then on every row until 33 sts rem. Cast off 3 sts at beg of next 6 rows. Cast off rem 15 sts.

FRONT BAND

Join shoulder seams.
With 2¾mm (No 12/US 2) needles, right side facing, A and beg at top of welt, pick up and k 66(74) sts up shaped edge of Right Front to shoulder, 29(33) sts across back neck and 66(74) sts down shaped edge of Left Front to top of welt. 161(181) sts. Beg with a 1st row, work 8 rows in rib as given for Back. Cast off in rib.

TIES (make 2)

With 2¾mm (No 12/US 2) needles and A, cast on 9 sts. Work 27(30)cm/10¾ (12)in in rib as given for Back. Cast off.

Fair Isle Ballet top with Sandals and Teddy

Chart 1

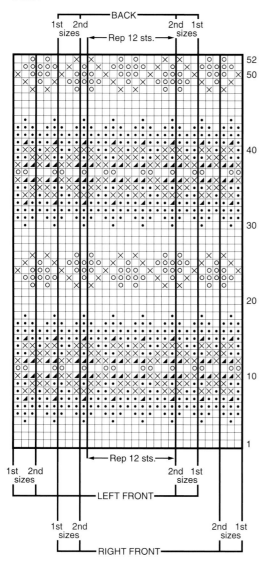

Chart 2

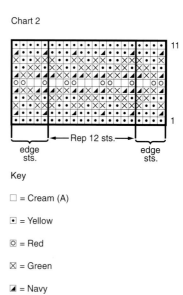

Key

☐ = Cream (A)

⊡ = Yellow

⊙ = Red

⊠ = Green

◪ = Navy

TO MAKE UP

Join sleeve seams and side seams, leaving small opening on welt at right seam. Sew in sleeves. Catch down short edges of front band to cast off sts on top of welt. Sew one end of ties to front welts.

Shoes

LEFT SHOE

With 2¾mm (No 12/US 2) needles and A, cast on 37(43) sts. K 1 row.
1st row K1, [m1, k17(20), m1, k1] twice.
2nd row and every foll alt row K.
3rd row K2, m1, k17(20), m1, k3, m1, k17(20), m1, k2.

5th row K3, m1, k17(20), m1, k5, m1, k17(20), m1, k3.
Cont in this way, inc 4 sts as set on every alt row until there are 61(71) sts. K 1 row.
Next row (right side) With Yellow, k6(4), m1, [k7, m1] 7(9) times, k6(4). 69(81) sts.
Beg with a p row and 2nd(1st) row of chart 2, work 9(11) rows in st st and patt from chart 2.
Next row With Yellow, k8(7), k2 tog, [k15(11), k2 tog] 3(5) times, k8(7). 65(75) sts.
Cont in A only.
Next row P37(42), p2 tog, turn.
Next row Sl 1, k9, skpo, turn.
Next row Sl 1, p9, p2 tog, turn.
Rep last 2 rows 5(7) times more, then work first of the 2 rows again.
Next row Sl 1, p to end.
Cast off purlwise, working 2 sts tog at each corner. Join back and sole seam. With 2¾mm (No 12/US 2) needles, right side facing, A and beg and ending within 10 sts of back seam, pick up and k21 sts along back heel. K 1 row.**
Next row Cast on 20(23), k to end, turn and cast on 4 sts.
K 1 row.
Buttonhole row K2, yf, skpo, k to end. K 2 rows. Cast off. Sew on button.

RIGHT SHOE

Work as given for Left Shoe to **.

Next row Cast on 4, k to end, turn and cast on 20(23) sts.
K 1 row.
Buttonhole row K to last 4 sts, k2 tog, yf, k2.
K 2 rows. Cast off. Sew on button.

Teddy

RIGHT LEG
With 3¼mm (No 10/US 3) needles and A, cast on 10 sts.
P 1 row.
Next row K1, [m1, k1] to end.
P 1 row.
Next row K7, m1, k1, m1, k8, m1, k1, m1, k2. 23 sts.
Work 3 rows in st st.
Next row K4, [skpo] twice, [k2 tog] twice, k11.
Next row P9, [p2 tog] twice, [p2 tog tbl] twice, p2.
Next row K3, k2 tog, k10. 14 sts.
** Work 11 rows in st st, inc one st at each end of 4th row.
Next row K1, k2 tog, k1, skpo, k3, k2 tog, k1, skpo, k2.
P 1 row.
Next row [K2 tog, k1, skpo, k1] twice.
Next row [P2 tog] to end.
Break off yarn, thread end through rem 4 sts, pull up and secure. Join sole and inner leg seam, leaving an opening. Stuff and close opening.

LEFT LEG
With 3¼mm (No 10/US 3) needles and A, cast on 10 sts.
P 1 row.
Next row K1, [m1, k1] to end.
P 1 row.
Next row K2, m1, k1, m1, k8, m1, k1, m1, k7. 23 sts.
Work 3 rows in st st.
Next row K11, [skpo] twice, [k2 tog] twice, k4.
Next row P2, [p2 tog] twice, [p2 tog tbl] twice, p9.
Next row K10, skpo, k3. 14 sts.
Complete as given for Right Leg from ** to end.

BODY
Begin at neck edge.
With 3¼mm (No 10/US 3) needles and A, cast on 15 sts.
P 1 row.

Next row K1, [m1, k1] to end. 29 sts.
Beg with a p row, work 5 rows in st st.
Next row [K7, m1] twice, k1, [m1, k7] twice.
Work 3 rows.
Next row K16, m1, k1, m1, k16. 35 sts.
Work 5 rows.
Next row K15, skpo, k1, k2 tog, k15.
Work 3 rows.
Next row K14, skpo, k1, k2 tog, k14.
Work 3 rows.
Next row K1, [k2 tog] to end. 16 sts.
P 1 row. Cast off.

ARMS (make 2)
With 3¼mm (No 10/US 3) needles and A, cast on 6 sts.
P 1 row.
Next row K1, [m1, k1] to end.
P 1 row.
Next row K1, [m1, k4, m1, k1] twice. 15 sts.
Work 3 rows.
Next row K1, [skpo, k2, k2 tog, k1] twice.
Work 13 rows in st st, inc one st at each end of 4th row. 13 sts.
Next row K1, [skpo, k1, k2 tog, k1] twice.
P 1 row.
Next row K1, [k2 tog] to end.
Break off yarn, thread end through rem 5 sts, pull up and secure. Join underarm seam, leaving an opening. Stuff and close opening.

HEAD
Begin at back.
With 3¼mm (No 10/US 3) needles and A, cast on 7 sts.
P 1 row.
Next row K1, [m1, k1] to end.
Rep last 2 rows once more. 25 sts.
Work 3 rows in st st.
Next row K1, [m1, k3] to end. 33 sts.
Work 13 rows.
Next row K1, [k2 tog] to end.
Work 3 rows.
Next row K1, [k2 tog] to end.
P 1 row. Break off yarn, thread end through rem 9 sts, pull up and secure. Join seam, leaving an opening. Stuff and close opening.

EARS (make 2)
With 3¼mm (No 10/US 3) needles and A, cast on 3 sts.
P 1 row.

Next row K1, [m1, k1] to end.
Rep last 2 rows once more. P 1 row.
Next row K1, m1, k2, m1, k3, m1, k2, m1, k1. 13 sts.
Work 5 rows in st st.
Next row [K1, skpo] twice, k1, [k2 tog, k1] twice.
P 1 row.
Next row [Skpo] twice, k1, [k2 tog] twice.
P 1 row.
Next row Skpo, k1, k2 tog.
Cast off.

DRESS
With 2¾mm (No 12/US 2) needles and B, cast on 76 sts.
K 5 rows.
Next row K.
Next row K3, p70, k3.
Rep last 2 rows 6 times.
Next row K3, [k2 tog] to last 3 sts, k3. 41 sts.
K 3 rows.
Next 2 rows Cast on 24 sts, k to end.
Next row Cast off 38 sts, k to end.
Next row Cast off 38 sts, k2 sts more, p7, k3.
Next row K6A, 1C, 6A.
Next row K3A, p2A, 3C, 2A, k3A.
Next row K4A, 5C, 4A.
Next row K3A, p2A, 1C, 1A, 1C, 2A, k3A.
With A, k 3 rows. Cast off.
With 2¾mm (No 12/US 2) needles and B, cast on 15 sts for strap. Cast off.
Make one more.
Sew straps in place. With C, embroider buttons.

TO MAKE UP
Fold sides of body to centre and join cast on edge. Gather neck edge, pull up and secure. Join back seam, leaving an opening. Stuff and close opening. Sew head in position. Fold ears in half widthwise and stitch together open edges. Sew ears in place. With Black, embroider nose, mouth and eyes. Attach yarn at seam about 1cm/¼in below top of one arm, thread yarn through body at shoulder position, then attach other arm, pull yarn tightly and thread through body again in same place, then attach to first arm again and fasten off. Attach legs at hip position in same way as arms.

Rosebud Cardigan, Shoes, Blanket and Teddy

See Pages
13, 19 & 22

Chart 1

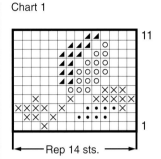

Rep 14 sts.

Chart 2

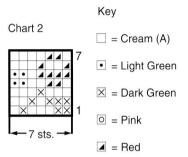

7 sts.

Key

☐ = Cream (A)

• = Light Green

☒ = Dark Green

◎ = Pink

◢ = Red

MATERIALS

Cardigan 4(5: 5) 50g balls of Rowan Cotton Glace in Cream (A).
1 ball of same in each of Light Green, Dark Green, Pink and Red.
Pair each of 3¼mm (No 10/US 3) and 3¾ mm (No 9/US 4) knitting needles.
5 buttons.
Shoes 1 50g ball of Rowan Cotton Glace in Cream (A).
Small amount of same in each of Light Green, Dark Green and Red.
Pair of 3mm (No 11/US 2) knitting needles.
2 buttons.
Blanket 7 50g balls of Rowan Cotton Glace in Cream (A).
1 ball of same in each of Light Green, Dark Green, Pink and Red.
Pair of 3¼mm (No 10/US 3) knitting needles.
Cable needle.
Teddy 1 50g ball of Rowan Cotton Glace in Cream (A).
Small amount of same in each of Light Green, Dark Green and Red.
Pair of 3mm (No 11/US 2) knitting needles.
Stuffing.

TENSION

23 sts and 32 rows to 10cm/4in square over st st on 3¾mm (No 9/US 4) needles.
25 sts and 34 rows to 10cm/4in square over st st on 3¼mm (No 10/US 3) needles.

MEASUREMENTS

Cardigan

To fit age	6	12	18	months
Actual chest	59	64	69	cm
measurements	23¼	25¼	27¼	in
Length	25	28	31	cm
	10	11	12¼	in
Sleeve seam	14	17	20	cm
	5½	6¾	8	in

Shoes

To fit age	6-12	12-18	months

Blanket

Approximately 55cm x 67cm/21½in x 26½ in.

Teddy

Approximately 18cm/7in high.

ABBREVIATIONS

C4F= sl next 2 sts onto cable needle and leave at front of work, k2, then k2 from cable needle.
Also see page 7.

NOTE

Read charts from right to left on right side rows and from left to right on wrong side rows unless otherwise stated. When working in pattern, use separate lengths of contrast colours for each coloured area and twist yarns together on wrong side at joins to avoid holes. If preferred, knit Teddy pieces in A only and swiss darn (see diagram page 68) all flower motifs afterwards.

Shape Shoulders

Cast off 8(8: 9) sts at beg of next 4 rows and 7(9: 9) sts at beg of next 2 rows. Leave rem 22(24: 26) sts on a holder.

LEFT FRONT

With 3¼mm (No 10/US 3) needles and A, cast on 31(35: 37) sts.
Work 2cm/¾in in moss st as given for Back, inc 1(0: 1) st at centre of last row. 32(35: 38) sts.
Change to 3¾mm (No 9/US 4) needles.
Beg with a k row, work 4(2: 0) rows in st st. **
1st row (right side) K0(21: 6)A, k14 sts of 1st row of chart 1, k18(0: 18)A.
2nd row P18(0: 18)A, p14 sts of 2nd row of chart 1, p0(21: 6)A.
3rd to 11th rows Rep last 2 rows 4 times then work first of the 2 rows again, but working 3rd to 11th rows of chart 1.
12th to 14th rows With A and beg with a p row, work 3 rows in st st.
15th row K18(3: 24)A, k14 sts of 1st row of chart 1, k0(18: 0)A.
16th row P0(18: 0)A, p14 sts of 2nd row of chart 1, p18(3: 24)A.
17th to 28th rows Work 3rd to 14th rows.

Cardigan

BACK

With 3¼mm (No 10/US 3) needles and A, cast on 67(73: 79) sts.
1st row K1, [p1, k1] to end.
This row forms moss st. Work 2cm/¾in in moss st, inc one st at centre of last row. 68(74: 80) sts.
Change to 3¾mm (No 9/US 4) needles.
Beg with a k row, work 4(2: 0) rows in st st.
1st row (right side) K0(21: 6)A, k14 sts of 1st row of chart 1, k22A, k14 sts of 1st row of chart 1, k18(3: 24)A.
2nd row P18(3: 24)A, p14 sts of 2nd row of chart 1, p22A, p14 sts of 2nd row of chart 1, p0(21: 6)A.
3rd to 11th rows Rep last 2 rows 4 times then work first of the 2 rows again, but working 3rd to 11th rows of chart 1.
12th to 14th rows With A and beg with a p row, work 3 rows in st st.
15th row K18(3: 24)A, k14 sts of 1st row of chart 1, k22A, k14 sts of 1st row of chart 1, k0(21: 6)A.
16th row P0(21: 6)A, p14 sts of 2nd row of chart 1, p22A, p14 sts of 2nd row of chart 1, p18(3: 24)A.
17th to 28th rows Work 3rd to 14th rows.
These 28 rows form patt. Patt a further 42(54: 66) rows.

56

These 28 rows form patt. Patt a further 31(43: 55) rows.

Shape Neck
Next row Patt 4(5: 6) and slip these sts onto a safety pin, patt to end.
Keeping patt correct, dec one st at neck edge on next 5 rows. 23(25: 27) sts. Patt 5 rows straight.

Shape Shoulder
Cast off 8(8: 9) sts at beg of next row and foll alt row. Work 1 row. Cast off rem 7(9: 9) sts.

RIGHT FRONT
Work as given for Left Front to **.
1st row (right side) K0(18: 0)A, k14 sts of 1st row of chart 1, k18(3: 24)A.
2nd row P18(3: 24)A, p14 sts of 2nd row of chart 1, p0(18: 0)A.
3rd to 11th rows Rep last 2 rows 4 times then work first of the 2 rows again, but working 3rd to 11th rows of chart 1.
12th to 14th rows With A and beg with a p row, work 3 rows in st st.
15th row K18(0: 18)A, k14 sts of 1st row of chart 1, k0(21: 6)A.
16th row P0(21: 6)A, p14 sts of 2nd row of chart 1, p18(0: 18)A.
17th to 28th rows Work 3rd to 14th rows.
These 28 rows form patt. Complete to match Left Front, reversing shapings.

SLEEVES
With 3¼mm (No 10/US 3) needles and A, cast on 35(39: 43) sts.
Work 2cm/¾in in moss st as given for Back, inc one st at centre of last row. 36(40: 44) sts.
Change to 3¾mm (No 9/US 4) needles. Beg with a k row, work 0(4: 2) rows in st st.
Next row (right side) With A, k twice in next st, k1(3: 23)A, k14 sts of 1st row of chart 1, k19(21: 5)A, with A, k twice in last st.
Work a further 10 rows as set, inc one st at each end of 2 foll 4th rows. With A and beg with a p row, work 3 rows in st st, inc one st at each end of 2nd row. 44(48: 52) sts.
Next row K24(26: 10)A, k14 sts of 1st row of chart 1, k6(8: 28)A.
Work a further 10 rows as set, inc one st at each end of 2nd row and 2 foll 4th rows. 50(54: 58) sts. With A and beg with a p row, work 3 rows in st st. The last 28 rows set patt. Patt 12(16: 28) rows more, inc one st at each end of 1st(1st: 3rd) row and foll 4th(6th: 6th) row. 54(58: 62) sts. Cast off.

BUTTON BAND
With 3¼mm (No 10/US 3) needles and A, cast on 7 sts. Work in moss st as given for Back until band, when slightly stretched, fits along front edge of Left Front, ending with a wrong side row. Leave these sts.
Sew band in place. Mark band to indicate position of 5 buttons: first one 1cm/½in up from lower edge, last one 1cm/½in down from neck edge and rem 3 evenly spaced between.

BUTTONHOLE BAND
Work to match Button Band, making buttonholes to match markers as follows:
Buttonhole row (right side) Moss st 3, yf, k2 tog, moss st 2.

COLLAR
Join shoulder seams.
With 3¼mm (No 10/US 3) needles, A and right side facing, cast off in moss st first 3 sts of buttonhole band, moss st 2 sts more, work 2 tog last st of band with first st on safety pin, k rem 3(4: 5) sts, pick up and k14 sts up right front neck, k back neck sts inc one st, pick up and k14 sts down left front neck, then k3(4: 5) sts from safety pin, work 2 tog last st with first st of button band, moss st rem 6 sts, turn and cast off in moss st first 3 sts. 65(69: 73) sts. Work 7 rows in moss st.
Change to 3¾mm (No 9/US 4) needles and work 13 more rows. Cast off loosely in moss st.

TO MAKE UP
Sew on sleeves, placing centre of sleeves to shoulder seams. Join side and sleeve seams. Sew on buttons.

Shoes

RIGHT SHOE
With 3mm (No 11/US 2) needles and A, cast on 34(40) sts.
K 1 row.
1st row (right side) K1, yf, k15(18), yf, [k1, yf] twice, k15(18), yf, k1.
2nd row and 4 foll alt rows K to end, working k tbl into yf of previous row.
3rd row K2, yf, k15(18), yf, k2, yf, k3, yf, k15(18), yf, k2.
5th row K3, yf, k15(18), yf, [k4, yf] twice, k15(18), yf, k3.
7th row K4, yf, k15(18), yf, k5, yf, k6, yf, k15(18), yf, k4.
9th row K5, yf, k15(18), yf, [k7, yf] twice, k15(18), yf, k5.
11th row K7, yf, [k9(10), yf] 5 times, k7(8). 65(71) sts.
12th row As 2nd row.
Next row K1, [p1, k1] to end.
Rep last row 11 times more.
Shape Instep
Next row Patt 26(29), k12, skpo, turn.

Next row Sl 1, p11, p2 tog, turn.
Next row Sl 1, k11, skpo, turn.
Rep last 2 rows once more then work first of the 2 rows again.
Next row Sl 1, k2A, k7 sts of first row of chart 2, k2A, with A, skpo, turn.
Next row Sl 1, p2A, p7 sts of 2nd row of chart 2, p2A, with A, p2 tog, turn.
Rep last 2 rows twice more then work first of the 2 rows again, but working 3rd to 7th rows of chart 2. Cont in A only.
Next row Sl 1, p11, p2 tog, turn.
Next row Sl 1, k11, skpo, turn.
Next row Sl 1, p11, p2 tog, turn.
Next row Sl 1, k12, patt to end.
Cast off in patt, dec one st at each corner. Join sole and back heel seam.
With 3mm (No 11/US 2) needles, A, right side facing and beginning and ending within 8 sts of back seam, pick up 17 sts along heel. K 1 row. **
Next row Cast on 3, k to end, turn and cast on 19 sts.
K 2 rows.
Buttonhole row K2, yf, k2 tog, k to end.
K 3 rows. Cast off. Sew on button.

LEFT SHOE
Work as given for Right Shoe to **, reversing motif by reading chart from left to right on right side rows and from right to left on wrong side rows.
Next row Cast on 19 sts, k to end, turn and cast on 3 sts.
K 2 rows.
Buttonhole row K to last 4 sts, skpo, yf, k2.
K3 rows. Cast off. Sew on button.

Blanket

With 3¼mm (No 10/US 3) needles and A, cast on 150 sts.
1st row (right side) P1, k1, p1, C4F, * p1, [k1, p1] 15 times, C4F; rep from * 3 times more, p1, k1, p1.
2nd row P1, k1, p6, * k1, [p1, k1]14 times, p6; rep from * 3 times more, k1, p1.
3rd row P1, k1, p1, k4, * p1, [k1, p1] 15 times, k4; rep from * 3 times more, p1, k1, p1.
4th row As 2nd row.
5th and 6th rows Work 1st and 2nd rows.
7th row P1, k1, p1, k4, p1, k1, p1, [k25, p1, k1, p1, k4, p1, k1, p1] 4 times.
8th row P1, k1, p6, k1, [p27, k1, p6, k1] 4 times, p1.
9th row P1, k1, p1, C4F, p1, k1, p1, [k25, p1, k1, p1, C4F, p1, k1, p1] 4 times.
10th row As 8th row.
11th and 12th rows As 7th and 8th rows.

13th row With A, p1, k1, p1, C4F, p1, k1, p1, [k2A, k7 sts of 1st row of chart 2, k7A, k7 sts of 1st row of chart 2, with A, k2, p1, k1, p1, C4F, p1, k1, p1, k25, p1, k1, p1, C4F, p1, k1, p1] twice.

14th row With A, p1, k1, p6, k1, p1, [with A, p26, k1, p6, k1, p3, p7 sts of 2nd row of chart 2, p7A, p7 sts of 2nd row of chart 2, with A, p3, k1, p6, k1, p1] twice.

15th row With A, p1, k1, p1, k4, p1, k1, p1, [k2A, k7 sts of 3rd row of chart 2, k7A, k7 sts of 3rd row of chart 2, with A, k2, p1, k1, p1, k4, p1, k25, p1, k1, p1, k4, p1, k1, p1] twice.

16th row As 14th row, but working 4th row of chart 2.

17th rows As 13th row, but working 5th row of chart 2.

18th row With A, p1, k1, p6, k1, p1, [p5A, p14 sts of 1st row of chart 1, with A, p7, k1, p6, k1, p3, p7 sts of 6th row of chart 2, p7A, p7 sts of 6th row of chart 2, with A, p3, k1, p6, k1, p1] twice.

19th row With A, p1, k1, p1, k4, p1, k1, p1, [k2A, k7 sts of 7th row of chart 2, k7A, k7 sts of 7th row of chart 2, with A, k2, p1, k1, p1, k4, p1, k1, p1, k6, k14 sts of 2nd row of chart 1, with A, k5, p1, k1, p1, k4, p1, k1, p1] twice.

20th row With A, p1, k1, p6, k1, p1, [p5A, p14 sts of 3rd row of chart 1, with A, p7, k1, p6, k1, p27, k1, p6, k1, p1] twice.

21st row With A, p1, k1, p1, C4F, p1, k1, p1, [with A, k25, p1, k1, p1, C4F, p1, k1, p1, k6, k14 sts of 4th row of chart 1, with A, k5, p1, k1, p1, C4F, p1, k1, p1] twice.

22nd row As 20th row, but working 5th row of chart 1.

23rd row With A, p1, k1, p1, k4, p1, k1, p1, [with A, k25, p1, k1, p1, k4, p1, k1, p1, k6, k14 sts of 6th row of chart 1, with A, k5, p1, k1, p1, k4, p1, k1, p1] twice.

24th to 27th rows Work 20th to 23rd rows, but working 7th to 10th rows of chart 1.

28th row With A, p1, k1, p6, k1, p1, [p5A, p14 sts of 11th row of chart 1, with A, p7, k1, p6, k1, p10A, p7 sts of 1st row of chart 2, p10, k1, p6, k1, p1] twice.

29th row With A, p1, k1, p1, C4F, p1, k1, p1, [k9A, k7 sts of 2nd row of chart 2, with A, k9, p1, k1, p1, C4F, p1, k1, p1, k25, p1, k1, p1, C4F, p1, k1, p1] twice.

30th row With A, p1, k1, p6, k1, p1, [with A, p26, k1, p6, k1, p10, p7 sts of 3rd row of chart 2, with A, p10, k1, p6, k1, p1] twice.

31st row With A, p1, k1, p1, k4, p1, k1, p1, [k9A, k7 sts of 4th row of chart 2,

with A, k9, p1, k1, p1, k4, p1, k1, p1, k25, p1, k1, p1, k4, p1, k1, p1] twice.

32nd row As 30th row, but working 5th row of chart 2.

33rd to 34th rows As 29th and 30th rows, but working 6th and 7th rows of chart 2.

35th to 40th rows With A, work 7th to 10th rows then 7th and 8th rows again.

41st to 52nd rows With A, work 1st to 12th rows.

53rd row With A, p1, k1, p1, C4F, p1, k1, p1, [with A, k25, p1, k1, p1, C4F, p1, k1, p1, k2, k7 sts of 1st row of chart 2, k7A, k7 sts of 1st row of chart 2, with A, k2, p1, k1, p1, C4F, p1, k1, p1] twice.

54th row With A, p1, k1, p6, k1, p1, [p2A, p7 sts of 2nd row of chart 2, p7A, p7 sts of 2nd row of chart 2, with A, p3, k1, p6, k1, p27, k1, p6, k1, p1] twice.

55th row With A, p1, k1, p1, k4, p1, k1, p1, [with A, k25, p1, k1, p1, k4, p1, k1, p1, k2, k7 sts of 3rd row of chart 2, k7A, k7 sts of 3rd row of chart 2, with A, k2, p1, k1, p1, k4, p1, k1, p1] twice.

56th row As 54th row, but working 4th row of chart 2.

57th row As 53rd row, but working 5th row of chart 2.

58th row With A, p1, k1, p6, k1, p1, [p2A, p7 sts of 6th row of chart 2, p7A, p7 sts of 6th row of chart 2, with A, p3, k1, p6, k1, p6, p14 sts of 1st row of chart 1, with A, p7, k1, p6, k1, p1] twice.

59th row With A, p1, k1, p1, k4, p1, k1, p1, [k6A, k14 sts of 2nd row of chart 1, with A, k5, p1, k1, p1, k4, p1, k1, p1, k2, k7 sts of 7th row of chart 2, k7A, k7 sts of 7th row of chart 2, with A, k2, p1, k1, p1, k4, p1, k1, p1] twice.

60th row With A, p1, k1, p6, k1, p1, [with A, p26, k1, p6, k1, p6, p14 sts of 3rd row of chart 1, with A, p7, k1, p6, k1, p1] twice.

61st row With A, p1, k1, p1, C4F, p1, k1, p1, [k6A, k14 sts of 4th row of chart 1, with A, k5, p1, k1, p1, C4F, p1, k1, p1, k25, p1, k1, p1, C4F, p1, k1, p1] twice.

62nd row As 60th row, but working 5th row of chart 1.

63rd row With A, p1, k1, p1, k4, p1, k1, p1, [k6A, k14 sts of 6th row of chart 1, with A, k5, p1, k1, p1, k4, p1, k1, p1, k25, p1, k1, p1, k4, p1, k1, p1] twice.

64th and 65th rows As 60th and 61st rows, but working 7th and 8th rows of chart 1.

66th row As 60th row, but working 9th row of chart 1.

67th row As 63rd row, but working 10th row of chart 1.

68th row With A, p1, k1, p6, k1, p1, [p9A, p7 sts of 1st row of chart 2, with A, p10, k1, p6, k1, p6, p14 sts of 11th row of chart 1, with A, p7, k1, p6, k1, p1] twice.

69th row With A, p1, k1, p1, C4F, p1, k1, p1, [with A, k25, p1, k1, p1, C4F, p1, k1, p1, k9, k7 sts of 2nd row of chart 2, with A, k9, p1, k1, p1, C4F, p1, k1, p1] twice.

70th row With A, p1, k1, p6, k1, p1, [p9A, p7 sts of 3rd row of chart 2, with A, p10, k1, p6, k1, p27, k1, p6, k1, p1] twice.

71st row With A, p1, k1, p1, k4, p1, k1, p1, [with A, k25, p1, k1, p1, k4, p1, k1, p1, k9, k7 sts of 4th row of chart 2, with A, k9, p1, k1, p1, k4, p1, k1, p1] twice.

72nd row As 70th row, but working 5th row of chart 2.

73rd and 74th rows Work 69th and 70th rows, but working 6th and 7th rows of chart 2.

75th to 80th rows Work 35th to 40th rows.

Rep these 80 rows twice more, then with A, work 1st to 6th rows. Cast off, working 2 sts tog over each cable.

Teddy

LEGS (make 2)
With 3mm (No 11/US 2) needles and A, cast on 25 sts.
P 1 row.
Next row K2A, k7 sts of 1st row of chart 2, k7A, k7 sts of 1st row of chart 2, k2A.
Next row P2A, p7 sts of 2nd row of chart 2, p7A, p7 sts of 2nd row of chart 2, p2A.
Work a further 5 rows as set.
Next row With A, p12, cast off next 10 sts, p to end.
With A, work 4 rows in st st across all sts.
Next row K4A, k7 sts of 1st row of chart 2, k4A.
Next row P4A, p7 sts of 2nd row of chart 2, p4A.
Work a further 5 rows as set. With A, work 3 rows. Cast off.

SOLES (make 2)
With 3mm (No 11/US 2) needles and A, cast on 9 sts.
Beg with a p row, work 3 rows in st st.
Next row K1A, k7 sts of 1st row of chart 2, k1A.
Next row P1A, p7 sts of 2nd row of chart 2, p1A.
Work a further 5 rows as set. With A, work 3 rows. Cast off.

BODY (make 2)

With 3mm (No 11/US 2) needles and A, cast on 16 sts.
Beg with a p row, work 3 rows in st st.
Next row K8A, k7 sts of 1st row of chart 2, k1A.
Next row P1A, p7 sts of 2nd row of chart 2, p8A.
Work a further 5 rows as set. With A, work 5 rows.
Next row K1A, k7 sts of 1st row of chart 2, k8A.
Next row P8A, p7 sts of 2nd row of chart 2, p1A.
Work a further 5 rows as set. With A, work 3 rows. Cast off.

ARMS (make 2)

With 3mm (No 11/US 2) needles and A, cast on 13 sts.
Beg with a p row, work 7 rows in st st.
Next row K3A, k7 sts of 1st row of chart 2, k3A.
Next row P3A, p7 sts of 2nd row of chart 2, p3A.
Work a further 5 rows as set. With A, work 7 rows. Cast off.

HEAD (make 2)

With 3mm (No 11/US 2) needles and A, cast on 15 sts.
Beg with a p row, work 5 rows in st st.
Next row K4A, k7 sts of 1st row of chart 2, k4A.
Next row P4A, p7 sts of 2nd row of chart 2, p4A.
Work a further 5 rows as set. With A, work 5 rows. Cast off.

EARS

With 3mm (No 11/US 2) needles and A, cast on 9 sts.
P 1 row.
Next row K1A, k7 sts of 1st row of chart 2, k1A.
Next row P1A, p7 sts of 2nd row of chart 2, p1A.
Work a further 5 rows as set. With A, p 1 row. Cast off.
Work one more piece in same way.
Using A only, make two more pieces in same way.

TO MAKE UP

Join instep seam on legs. Rounding seam at top, join top and back leg seam, leaving an opening. Sew in soles, rounding corners. Stuff and close opening. Make darts at centre of lower and top edges of body pieces, making top darts longer. With right sides together, join body pieces, tapering corners and leaving top edge open. Turn to right side and stuff firmly. Gather top edge, pull up and secure. Fold arms in half lengthwise and join seams, tapering corners and leaving an opening. Stuff firmly and close opening. With right sides of head pieces together and leaving cast on edge free, sew around pieces, tapering corners and forming point at centre front edge for nose. Turn to right side and stuff firmly. Gather open edge, pull up and secure. Sew head in place. Attach yarn 1cm/⅜in down from top at centre of one arm, thread through body at shoulder position, attach other arm, then thread yarn through body in same place again, pull up tightly, attach to first arm again and fasten off. Attach legs at hip position in same way as arms. With right side of paired ear pieces together, work seam around, tapering corners and leaving cast on edge free. Turn to right side and close opening. Sew them in place.

Twinset with Fair Isle Border

See Pages 23 & 25

MATERIALS

For the set 6 50g balls of Rowan True 4 ply Botany in Light Pink (A).
1 ball of same in each of Cream, Dark Blue, Light Blue, Yellow and Red.
Pair each of 3mm (No 11/US 2) and 3¼ mm (No 10/US 3) knitting needles.
9 buttons.

TENSION

28 sts and 36 rows to 10cm/4in square over st st on 3¼mm (No 10/US 3) needles.

ABBREVIATIONS

See page 7.

NOTE

Read chart from right to left on right side (k) rows and from left to right on wrong side (p) rows. When working in pattern, strand yarn not in use loosely across wrong side to keep fabric elastic.

MEASUREMENTS

To fit age	12-18 months
Cardigan	
Actual chest	62 cm
measurement	24½ in
Length	30 cm
	11¾ in
Sleeve seam	23 cm
	9 in
sweater	
Actual chest	55 cm
measurement	21½ in
Length	28 cm
	11 in
Sleeve seam	7 cm
	2¾ in

Cardigan

BACK

With 3mm (No 11/US 2) needles and A, cast on 85 sts.
1st rib row (right side) K1, [p1, k1] to end.
2nd rib row P1, [k1, p1] to end.
Rep last 2 rows 5 times more.
Change to 3¼mm (No 10/US 3) needles.
Beg with a k row, work 4 rows in st st.
Work in st st and patt from chart until 15th row of chart has been worked.
Cont in A only until Back measures 17cm/6¾in from beg, ending with a p row.

Shape Armholes

Cast off 2 sts at beg of next 8 rows. 69 sts. Cont straight until Back measures 30cm/11¾in from beg, ending with a p row.

Shape Shoulders

Cast off 9 sts at beg of next 2 rows and 10 sts at beg of foll 2 rows. Leave rem 31 sts on a holder.

RIGHT FRONT

With 3mm (No 11/US 2) needles and A, cast on 49 sts.

1st rib row (right side) K2, p1, [k1, p1] to end.

2nd rib row K1, [p1, k1] to end.

Rib 2 rows more.

Buttonhole row (right side) Rib 3, yrn, p2 tog, rib to end.

Rib 6 rows more.

Next row Rib to last 6 sts, turn: leave the 6 sts on a safety pin. 43 sts.

Change to 3¼mm (No 10/US 3) needles. Beg with a k row, work 4 rows in st st. Work in st st and patt from chart until 15th row of chart has been worked. Cont in A only until Front matches Back to armhole shaping, ending with a k row.

Shape Armhole

Cast off 2 sts at beg of next row and 3 foll alt rows. 35 sts. Cont straight until Front measures 26cm/10¼in from beg, ending with a p row.

Shape Neck

Next row K7 and slip these 7 sts onto a safety pin, k to end.

Work 1 row. Cast off 3 sts at beg of next row and 2 sts at beg of foll alt row. Dec one st at neck edge on every row until 19 sts rem. Cont straight until Front matches Back to shoulder shaping, ending with a k row.

Shape Shoulder

Cast off 9 sts at beg of next row. Work 1 row. Cast off rem 10 sts.

LEFT FRONT

With 3mm (No 11/US 2) needles and A, cast on 49 sts.

1st rib row (right side) P1, [k1, p1] to last 2 sts, k2.

2nd rib row K1, [p1, k1] to end.

Rib 9 rows more.

Next row Rib 6 and slip these 6 sts onto a safety pin, rib to end. 43 sts. Change to 3¼mm (No 10/US 3) needles. Complete to match Right Front, reversing shapings.

SLEEVES

With 3mm (No 11/US 2) needles and A, cast on 47 sts.

Work 14 rows in rib as given for Back. Change to 3¼mm (No 10/US 3) needles. Beg with a k row, work 4 rows in st st, inc one st at each end of 3rd row. 49 sts. Work 15 rows of patt from chart as indicated for Back, **at the same time,** inc one st at each end of 3rd row and 3 foll 4th rows, working inc sts into patt. 57 sts. Cont in A only, inc one st at each end of every foll 4th row until there are 75 sts. Work straight until Sleeve measures 23cm/9in from beg, ending with a p row.

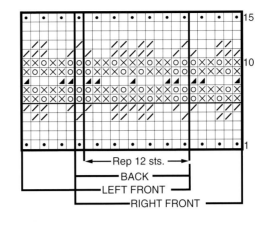

←— Rep 12 sts. —→
BACK
LEFT FRONT
RIGHT FRONT

Key

• = Light Pink (A)

☐ = Cream

⟋ = Dark Blue

☒ = Light Blue

◻ = Yellow

◣ = Red

Shape Top

Cast off 2 sts at beg of next 8 rows. Cast off rem 59 sts.

BUTTON BAND

With 3mm (No 11/US 2) needles, rejoin A yarn at inside edge to the 6 sts of Left Front welt, cast on 1 st, rib to end. Cont in rib until band, when slightly stretched, fits along front edge to neck edge, ending at inside edge. Leave these sts on a safety pin. Sew band in place. Mark position for 6 buttons: first one to match buttonhole already made on Right Front, last one to be worked on 4th row of neckband and rem 4 evenly spaced between.

BUTTONHOLE BAND

Work to match Button Band, making buttonholes at markers as before and ending at outside edge. Leave sts on needle.

NECKBAND

Join shoulder seams.

With 3mm (No 11/US 2) needles, A and right side facing, rib first 6 sts of buttonhole band, work last st tog with first st of neck shaping, k rem 6 sts, pick up and k 14 sts up right front neck, k back neck sts, pick up and k14 sts down left front neck, k first 6 sts of front neck shaping, work last st tog with first st of button band, rib rem 6 sts. 85 sts. Rib 6 rows, making buttonhole on 4th row. Cast off in rib.

TO MAKE UP

Sew on sleeves, placing centre of sleeves to shoulder seams. Join side and sleeve seams. Sew on buttons.

Sweater

BACK

With 3mm (No 11/US 2) needles and A, cast on 77 sts.

1st rib row (right side) K1, [p1, k1] to end.

2nd rib row P1, [k1, p1] to end.

Rib 10 rows more.

Change to 3¼mm (No 10/US 3) needles. Beg with a k row, work in st st until Back measures 16cm/6¼in from beg, ending with a p row.

Shape Armholes

Cast off 2 sts at beg of next 8 rows. 61 sts. Work 2 rows.

Work in patt from chart until 15th row of chart has been worked. Cont in A only, work 3 rows.**

Divide for Opening

Next row K28, turn.

Work on this set of sts only until Back measures 28cm/11in from beg, ending at armhole edge.

Shape Shoulder

Cast off 7 sts at beg of next row and 8 sts at beg of foll alt row. Leave rem 13 sts on a holder.

With right side facing, slip centre 5 sts onto a safety pin, rejoin yarn to rem sts and k to end. Complete as given for first side.

FRONT

Work as given for Back to **.

Shape Neck

Next row K22, turn.

Work on this set of sts only. Cast off 3 sts at beg of next row. Dec one st at neck edge on every alt row until 15 sts rem. Cont straight until Front matches Back to shoulder shaping, ending at armhole edge.

Shape Shoulder

Cast off 7 sts at beg of next row. Work 1 row. Cast off rem 8 sts.
With right side facing, slip centre 17 sts onto a holder, rejoin yarn to rem sts, k to end. P 1 row. Complete as given for first side.

SLEEVES

With 3mm (No 11/US 2) needles and A, cast on 60 sts. Work 4 rows in k1, p1 rib.
Change to 3¼mm (No 10/US 3) needles. Beg with a k row, work 22 rows in st st, inc one st at each end of 3rd row and 4 foll 4th rows. 70 sts.

Shape Top

Cast off 2 sts at beg of next 8 rows.
Cast off rem 54 sts.

BUTTON BAND

With 3mm (No 11/US 2) needles and A, cast on 7 sts.

1st rib row (right side) P1, [k1, p1] twice, k2.
2nd rib row K1, [p1, k1] 3 times. Rep last 2 rows 7 times more. Leave these sts on a safety pin.

BUTTONHOLE BAND

With 3mm (No 11/US 2) needles and right side facing, rejoin yarn to sts at base of back opening, k2, m1, k2, k twice in next st. 7 sts.
1st rib row K1, [p1, k1] 3 times.
2nd rib row K2, [p1, k1] twice, p1.
Rib 3 rows more.
Buttonhole row Rib 3, yrn , p2 tog, rib 2.
Rep last 6 rows once more. Rib 3 rows more. Leave sts on needle.

NECKBAND

Join shoulder seams. Sew on buttonhole band to left side of opening and button band to right side. Catch down cast on sts of button band on wrong side at base of opening.
With 3mm (No 11/US 2) needles, right side facing and A, rib the 6 sts of buttonhole band, work last st tog with first st of back neck sts, k rem 12 sts, pick up and k14 sts down left front neck, k centre front sts, pick up and k14 sts up right front neck, k first 12 sts of back neck, work last st tog with first st of button band, rib rem 6 sts. 83 sts.
Work 6 rows in rib, making buttonhole on 2nd row. Cast off in rib.

TO MAKE UP

Sew on sleeves, placing centre of sleeves to shoulder seams. Join side and sleeve seams. Sew on buttons.

A B C Sweater and Blanket

See Pages 19, 26 & 27

MATERIALS

Sweater 5 50g balls of Rowan DK Handknit Cotton.
Pair each of 3¼mm (No 10/US 3) and 4mm (No 8/US 6) knitting needles.
Cable needle.
4 buttons.
Blanket 13 50g balls of Rowan DK Handknit Cotton.
Pair of 4mm (No 8/US 6) knitting needles.
Cable needle.

TENSION

20 sts and 28 rows to 10cm/4in square over st st on 4mm (No 8/US 6) needles.

MEASUREMENTS

Sweater

To fit age	9-12 months
Actual chest measurement	60 cm
	23½ in
Length	31 cm
	12¼ in
Sleeve seam	18 cm
	7 in

Blanket
Approximately 74cm x 107cm/29in x 42in.

ABBREVIATIONS

See page 7.

PANEL A

Worked over 13 sts.
1st row (right side) K1, p11, k1.
2nd row P1, k11, p1.
3rd row K13.
4th row P13.
5th row K13.
6th row P6, k1, p6.
7th row K5, p1, k1, p1, k5.
8th row P4, k1, [p1, k1] twice, p4.
9th row K3, p1, [k1, p1] 3 times, k3.
10th row P2, k1, [p1, k1] 4 times, p2.
11th row As 9th row.
12th row As 8th row.
13th row As 7th row.
14th row As 6th row.
15th to 18th rows Rep 3rd and 4th rows twice.
These 18 rows form patt.

PANEL B

Worked over 4 sts.
1st row (right side) K4.
2nd row P4.
3rd and 4th rows As 1st and 2nd rows.
5th row Sl next 2 sts onto cable needle and leave at back, k2, then k2 from cable needle.
6th row P4.
These 6 rows form patt.

PANEL C

Worked over 13 sts.
1st row (right side) K1, p11, k1.
2nd row P1, k11, p1.
3rd row K13.
4th row P13.
5th row K5, p4, k4.
6th row P3, k6, p4.
7th row K3, p2, k3, p3, k2.
8th row P2, k2, p5, k1, p3.
9th row K9, p2, k2.
10th row P2, k2, p9.
11th and 12th rows As 9th and 10th rows.
13th row K3, p1, k5, p2, k2.
14th row P2, k3, p3, k2, p3.
15th row K4, p6, k3.
16th row P4, k4, p5.
17th row K13.
18th row P13.
19th to 22nd rows Work 1st to 4th rows.
23rd row K4, p7, k2.
24th row P2, k8, p3.
25th row K3, p2, k5, p1, k2.
26th row P2, k1, p5, k2, p3.

27th row As 25th row.
28th row P2, k7, p4.
29th row K5, p6, k2.
30th row P2, k1, p4, k2, p4.
31st row K3, p2, k5, p1, k2.
32nd row P2, k1, p5, k2, p3.
33rd row As 23rd row.
34th row P2, k6, p5.
35th to 40th rows Work 17th to 22nd rows.
41st row K1, p2, k7, p2, k1.
42nd row P1, k2, p7, k2, p1.
43rd row K2, p2, k5, p2, k2.
44th row P2, k9, p2.
45th row K3, p7, k3.
46th row P3, [k2, p3] twice.
47th row K4, p2, k1, p2, k4.
48th row P4, k2, p1, k2, p4.
49th row K5, p3, k5.
50th row P5, k3, p5.
51st row K6, p1, k6.
52nd row P6, k1, p6.
53rd and 54th rows As 17th and 18th rows.
These 54 rows form patt.

Sweater

BACK

With 3¼mm (No 10/US 3) needles, cast on 63 sts.
1st row P1, [k1, p1] to end.
This row forms moss st. Rep this row 3 times more.
Change to 4mm (No 8/US 6) needles.
Next row (right side) Moss st 3, k57, moss st 3.
Next row Moss st 3, p57, moss st 3.
Rep last 2 rows twice more.
Beg with a k row, work 21 rows in st st across all sts.
Inc row P21, [m1, p21] twice. 65 sts.
Work in patt as follows:
1st row (right side) P1, k1, p1, work 1st row of panel A, p1, k1, p1, work 1st row of panel B, p1, k1, p1, work 1st row of panel C, p1, k1, p1, work 1st row of panel B, p1, k1, p1, work 1st row of panel A, p1, k1, p1.

This row sets positions of panels and forms moss st between panels. Patt 57 rows more.
Shape Neck
Next row Patt 26, turn.
Work on this set of sts only. Dec one st at neck edge on next 5 rows. 21 sts.**
Cast off.
With right side facing, slip centre 13 sts onto a holder, rejoin yarn to rem sts, patt to end. Dec one st at neck edge on next 5 rows. 21 sts. Work 3 rows in moss st across all sts. Cast off in moss st.

FRONT

Work as given for Back to **. Work 1 row in moss st.
Buttonhole row Moss st 3, [yrn, p2 tog, moss st 4] 3 times.
Moss st 1 row. Cast off in moss st.
With right side facing, slip centre 13 sts onto a holder, rejoin yarn to rem sts, patt to end. Dec one st at neck edge on next 5 rows. Cast off.

SLEEVES

With 3¼mm (No 10/US 3) needles cast on 33 sts. Work 6 rows in moss st as given for Back.
Change to 4mm (No 8/US 6) needles. Beg with a k row, work 31 rows in st st, inc one st at each end of 3rd row and 7 foll 4th rows. 49 sts.
Inc row P14, m1, p21, m1, p14. 51 sts.
Work in patt as follows:
1st row P8, k1 (last 9 sts of 1st row of panel A), p1, k1, p1, work 1st row of panel B, p1, k1, p1, work 1st row of panel A, p1, k1, p1, work 1st row of panel B, p1, k1, p1, k1, p8 (first 9 sts of 1st row of panel A).
This row sets positions of panels and forms moss st between panels. Patt 19 rows more, inc one st at each end of 2nd row and 3 foll 4th rows, working inc sts into panel A patt. 59 sts.
Cast off.

NECKBAND

Join right shoulder seam. With 3¼mm (No 10/US 3) needles and right side facing, pick up and k12 sts down left front neck, k centre front sts, pick up and k9 sts up right front neck, 9 sts down right back neck, k centre back sts and dec one st, pick up and k12 sts up left back neck. 67 sts. Work 2 rows in moss st as given for Back.
Buttonhole row Moss st to last 4 sts, k2 tog, yf, moss st 2.
Work 2 rows in moss st. Cast off in moss st.

TO MAKE UP

Lap buttonhole border over button border on left shoulder and catch together at side edge. Sew on sleeves, placing centre of sleeves at shoulders. Join sleeve seams and side seams to top of moss st borders at lower edges. Sew on buttons.

Blanket

With 4mm (No 8/US 6) needles cast on 151 sts.
1st row P1, [k1, p1] to end.
This row forms moss st. Rep last row twice more.
Inc row Moss st 21, [m1, moss st 22] 5 times, m1, moss st 20. 157 sts.
Work in patt as follows:
1st row (right side) P1, k1, p1, [work 3rd row of panel A, p1, k1, p1, work 3rd row of panel B, p1, k1, p1, work 3rd row of panel C, p1, k1, p1, work 3rd row of panel B, p1, k1, p1] 3 times, work 3rd row of panel A, p1, k1, p1.
This row sets positions of panels and forms moss st between panels. Patt 321 rows more.
Dec row Moss st 20, [work 2 tog, moss st 21] 5 times, work 2 tog, moss st 20. 151 sts.
Work 3 rows in moss st. Cast off in moss st.

Bo Peep Sweater

See Page
27

MATERIALS
7 50g balls of Rowan Cotton Glace in Beige (A).
1 ball of same in each of Dark Navy, White and Brown.
Small amount of same in each of Red, Blue, Yellow and Pink.
Pair each of 2¾mm (No 12/US 2) and 3¼mm (No 10/US 3) needles.
Cable needle.

MEASUREMENTS

To fit age	2-3	years
Actual chest	66	cm
measurement	26	in
Length	39	cm
	15¼	in
Sleeve seam	23	cm
	9	in

TENSION
26 sts and 42 rows to 10cm/4in square over pattern on 3¼mm (No 10/US 3) needles.

ABBREVIATIONS
C4F = sl next 2 sts onto cable needle and leave at front of work, k2, then k2 from cable needle;
mk = make knot, [k1, p1, k1, p1, k1] all in next st, then pass 2nd, 3rd, 4th and 5th st over 1st st.
Also see page 7.

NOTE
Read charts from right to left on right side rows and from left to right on wrong side rows. When working colour motifs, use separate lengths of contrast colours for each coloured area and twist yarns together on wrong side at joins to avoid holes.

BACK
With 2¾mm (No 12/US 2) needles and A, cast on 86 sts.
1st rib row (right side) P2, mk, p2, [k4, p2, mk, p2] to end.
2nd rib row K5, [p4, k5] to end.
3rd rib row P5, [k4, p5] to end.
4th rib row As 2nd row.
Rib 10 rows more.
Change to 3¼mm (No 10/US 3) needles.
1st to 4th rows K.
5th row K.
6th row K5, [p4, k5] to end.
7th and 8th rows As 5th and 6th rows.
9th row K2, mk, k2, [C4F, k2, mk, k2] to end.
10th row As 6th row.
11th and 12th rows As 5th and 6th rows.
These 12 rows form patt. Patt 4 rows.
Next row With A, patt 14, work 22 sts of 1st row of chart 1, with A, patt 50.
Next row With A, patt 50, work 22 sts of 2nd row of chart 1, with A, patt 14.
Work a further 10 rows as set.
Next row With A, patt 14, work 22 sts of 13th row of chart 1, with A, patt 32, work 13 sts of 1st row of chart 2, with A, patt 5.
Next row With A, patt 5, work 13 sts of 2nd row of chart 2, with A, patt 32, work 22 sts of 14th row of chart 1, with A, patt 14.
Work a further 6 rows as set. With A, patt 16 rows across all sts.

Next row With A, patt 50, work 22 sts of 1st row of chart 3, with A, patt 14.
Next row With A, patt 14, work 22 sts of 2nd row of chart 3, with A, patt 50.
Work a further 10 rows as set.
Next row With A, patt 14, work 13 sts of 1st row of chart 4, with A, patt 23, work 22 sts of 13th row of chart 3, with A, patt 14.
Next row With A, patt 14, work 22 sts of 14th row of chart 3, with A, patt 23, work 13 sts of 2nd row of chart 4, with A, patt 14.
Work a further 6 rows as set. With A, patt 16 rows across all sts.
Next row With A, patt 23, work 22 sts of 1st row of chart 5, with A, patt 41.
Next row With A, patt 41, work 22 sts of 2nd row of chart 5, with A, patt 23.
Work a further 10 rows as set.
Next row With A, patt 23, work 22 sts of 13th row of chart 5, with A, patt 14, work 13 sts of 1st row of chart 6, with A, patt 14.
Next row With A, patt 14, work 13 sts of 2nd row of chart 6, with A, patt 14, work 22 sts of 14th row of chart 5, with A, patt 23.
Work a further 6 rows as set.
Next row With A, patt 23, work 22 sts of 21st row of chart 5, with A, patt 41.
Next row With A, patt 41, work 22 sts of 22nd row of chart 5, with A, patt 23.
Work a further 10 rows as set.** With A, patt 16 rows across all sts.

Next row With A, patt 5, work 13 sts of 1st row of chart 7, with A, patt 68.
Next row With A, patt 68, work 13 sts of 2nd row of chart 7, with A, patt 5.
Work a further 6 rows as set. Cont in A only, patt 2 rows across all sts.
Shape Shoulders
Next row Cast off 24, patt to last 24 sts, cast off last 24 sts.
Leave rem 38 sts on a holder.

FRONT
Work as given for Back to **. With A, patt 6 rows across all sts.
Shape Neck
Next row Patt 29, turn.
Work on this set of sts only. Keeping patt correct, dec one st at neck edge on next row and 4 foll alt rows. 24 sts.
Next row With A, patt 5, work 13 sts of 1st row of chart 7, with A, patt 6.
Next row With A, patt 6, work 13 sts of 2nd row of chart 7, with A, patt 5.
Work a further 6 rows as set. Cont in A only, patt 2 rows. Cast off.
With right side facing, slip centre 28 sts onto a holder, rejoin A yarn to rem sts and patt to end. Dec one st at neck edge on next row and 4 foll alt rows. Patt 10 rows straight. Cast off.

SLEEVES
With 2¾mm (No 12/US 2) needles and A, cast on 54 sts.
1st rib row (right side) K2, p2, mk, p2, [k4, p2, mk, p2] to last 2 sts, k2.
2nd rib row P2, k5, [p4, k5] to last 2 sts, p2.
3rd rib row K2, p5, [k4, p5] to last 2 sts, k2.
4th rib row As 2nd row.
Rib 10 rows more, inc one st at each end of last row. 56 sts.
Change to 3¼mm (No 10/US 3) needles.
1st to 4th rows K.
5th row With A, k twice in first st, k25, work 13 sts of 1st row of chart 4, with A, k16, k twice in last st.
6th row With A, [p4, k5] twice, work 13 sts of 2nd row of chart 4, with A, [k5, p4] 3 times.
7th row With A, k27, work 13 sts of 3rd row of chart 4, with A, k18.
8th row As 6th row but working 4th row of chart 4.
9th row With A, [C4F, k2, mk, k2] 3 times, work 13 sts of 5th row of chart 4, with A, [k2, mk, k2, C4F] twice.
10th row As 6th row but working 6th row of chart 4.

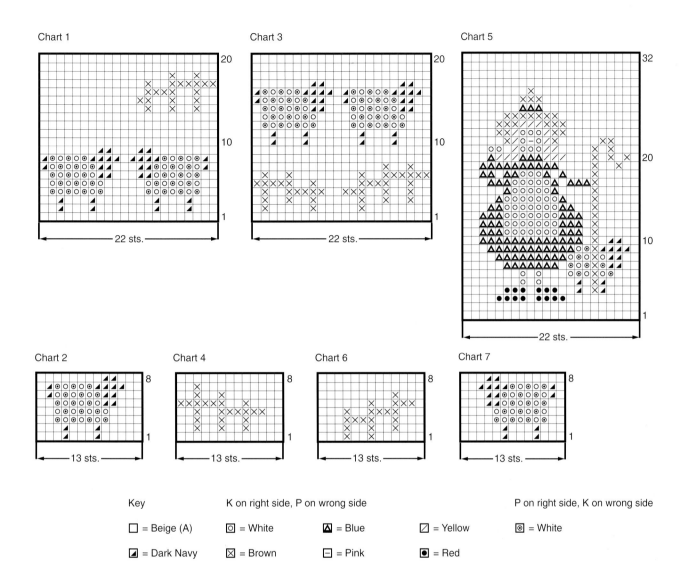

Chart 1

20

10

1

——— 22 sts. ———

Chart 3

20

10

1

——— 22 sts. ———

Chart 5

32

20

10

1

——— 22 sts. ———

Chart 2

8

1

—— 13 sts. ——

Chart 4

8

1

—— 13 sts. ——

Chart 6

8

1

—— 13 sts. ——

Chart 7

8

1

—— 13 sts. ——

Key

K on right side, P on wrong side

P on right side, K on wrong side

□ = Beige (A)

◉ = White   ▲ = Blue   ⧄ = Yellow   ◉ = White

◢ = Dark Navy   ⊠ = Brown   ⊟ = Pink   ◼ = Red

11th row With A, k twice in first st, k26, work 13 sts of 7th row of chart 4, with A, k17, k twice in last st.
12th row With A, k1, [p4, k5] twice, work 13 sts of 8th row of chart 4, with A, [k5, p4] 3 times, k1.
The last 12 rows set the patt. With A, patt 16 rows across all sts, inc one st at each end of 5th row and foll 6th row. 64 sts.
Next row With A, inc in first st, patt 11, work 13 sts of 1st row of chart 7, with A, patt 38, inc in last st.
Next row With A, patt 40, work 13 sts of 2nd row of chart 7, with A, patt 13.
Work a further 6 rows as set, inc one st at each end of 5th row. 68 sts. With A, patt 4 rows.
Next row With A, inc in first st, patt 40,

work 13 sts of 1st row of chart 2, with A, patt 13, inc in last st.
Next row With A, patt 15, work 13 sts of 2nd row of chart 2, with A, patt 42. Work a further 6 rows as set, inc one st at each end of 5th row. With A, patt 16 rows across all sts, inc one st at each end of 5th row and foll 6th row. 76 sts.
Next row With A, inc in first st, patt 26, work 13 sts of 1st row of chart 6, with A, patt 35, inc in last st. 78 sts.
Next row With A, patt 37, work 13 sts of 2nd row of chart 6, with A, patt 28. Work a further 6 rows as set. With A, patt 10 rows. Cast off.

NECKBAND
Join right shoulder seam.
With 2¾mm (No 12/US 2) needles, A

and right side facing, pick up and k23 sts down left front neck, k centre front neck sts, pick up and k21 sts up right front neck, k back neck sts. 110 sts.
1st rib row P3, [k5, p4] to last 8 sts, k5, p3.
2nd rib row K3, p5, [k4, p5] to last 3 sts, k3.
3rd rib row As 1st row.
4th rib row K3, p2, mk, p2, [k4, p2, mk, p2] to last 3 sts, k3.
Rib 9 rows more. Cast off in rib.

TO MAKE UP
Join left shoulder and neckband seam. Sew on sleeves, placing centre of sleeves to shoulder seams. Join side and sleeve seams. With Pink, embroider a bow on Bo Peep's crooks.

Duck Jacket

See Page
28

MATERIALS

3 50g balls of Rowan Designer DK Wool in Navy (A).
1 ball of same in each of Rust, Bright Green, Dark Blue, Red, Yellow, Cream and Light Blue.
Pair each of 3¼mm (No 10/US 3) and 4mm (No 8/US 6) knitting needles.
5 buttons.

MEASUREMENTS

To fit age	2	years
Actual chest	66	cm
measurement	26	in
Length	30	cm
	12	in
Sleeve seam	20	cm
	8	in

TENSION

26 sts and 28 rows to 10cm/4in square over Fair Isle pattern on 4mm (No 8/US 6) needles.

ABBREVIATIONS

See page 7.

NOTE

Read charts from right to left on right side (k) rows and from left to right on wrong side (p) rows. When working in pattern from chart 1, use separate lengths of contrast yarns for each coloured area and twist yarns together on wrong side at joins to avoid holes. On tartan band of pattern, the vertical line in Bright Green can be swiss darned (see diagram page 68) when the garment is completed. When working in pattern from charts 2 and 3, strand yarn not in use loosely across wrong side over no more than 5 sts at the time to keep fabric elastic.

Shape Shoulders

Cont in A only. Cast off 14 sts at beg of next 2 rows and 15 sts at beg of foll 2 rows. Leave rem 28 sts on a holder.

Left Front

With right side facing, rejoin yarn to rem sts and complete to match Right Front, reversing shapings.

SLEEVES

With 3¼mm (No 10/US 3) needles and A, cast on 50 sts.
Work 12 rows in k1, p1 rib.
Change to 4mm (No 8/US 6) needles.
Beg with a k row, work 2 rows in st st.
Cont in st st and yoke patt, inc one st at each end of next row and 3 foll alt rows, then on every foll 4th row until there are 72 sts, working inc sts into patt. Patt 7 rows straight. Cast off.

BUTTONHOLE BAND

With 3¼mm (No 10/US 3) needles, A and right side facing, pick up and k55 sts along straight right front edge. Rib

BACK AND FRONTS

Worked in one piece to armholes.
With 3¼mm (No 10/US 3) needles and A, cast on 169 sts.
1st rib row (right side) P1, [k1, p1] to end.
2nd rib row K1, [p1, k1] to end.
Rep last 2 rows once more, inc one st at centre of last row. 170 sts.
Change to 4mm (No 8/US 6) needles.
Beg with a k row, work in st st and patt from chart 1 until 40th row of chart 1 has been worked. Working 1st to 7th rows of chart 2 then 1st to 11th rows of chart 3 for yoke patt, cont in yoke patt, work 6 rows.

Right Front

Next row Patt 43, turn.
Work on this set of sts only. Patt 15 rows.

Shape Neck

Keeping patt correct, cast off 8 sts at beg of next row. Dec one st at neck edge on next 3 rows, then on 3 foll alt rows. 29 sts. Patt 11 rows straight.

Shape Shoulder

Cont in A only. Cast off 14 sts at beg of next row. Work 1 row. Cast off rem sts.

Back

With right side facing, rejoin yarn to rem sts, inc in first st, patt 82, inc in next st, turn. Work on this set of 86 sts for 35 rows.

Chart 1

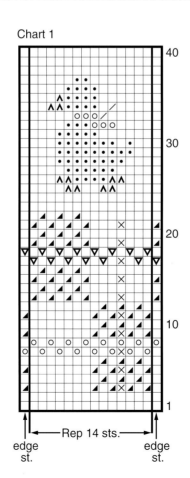

40

30

20

10

1

Rep 14 sts.

edge st.   edge st.

Chart 2

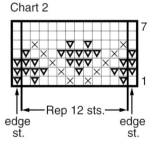

7

1

Rep 12 sts.

edge st.   edge st.

Chart 3

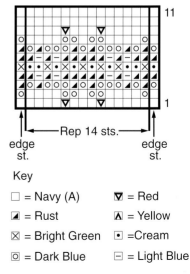

11

1

Rep 14 sts.

edge st.   edge st.

Key

□ = Navy (A)	▽ = Red
◸ = Rust	⋀ = Yellow
⊠ = Bright Green	• = Cream
⊚ = Dark Blue	⊟ = Light Blue

2nd row of Back and Fronts.
Buttonhole row Rib 3, yrn, p2 tog, [rib 10, yrn, p2 tog] 4 times, rib 2.
Rib 2 rows. Cast off in rib.

BUTTON BAND
Work to match Buttonhole Band omitting buttonholes.

NECKBAND
Join shoulder seams.
With 3¼mm (No 10/US 3) needles, A and right side facing, pick up and k31 sts up right front edge, omitting buttonhole band, k back neck sts dec one st at centre, pick up and k31 sts down left front neck, omitting button band. 89 sts.
Working in rib as given for Back and Fronts, cont as follows:
Next 2 rows Rib to last 16 sts, turn, sl 1, rib to last 16 sts, turn.
Next 2 rows Sl 1, rib to last 14 sts, turn.
Cont in this way, working 2 sts more at end of next 12 rows.
Next row Sl 1, rib to end.
Rib 1 row across all sts.
Next 2 rows Rib to last 2 sts, turn, sl 1, rib to last 2 sts, turn.
Next 2 rows Sl 1, rib to last 4 sts, turn.
Cont in this way, working 2 sts less at end of next 10 rows.
Next row Sl 1, rib to end.
Rib 1 row across all sts. Cast off loosely in rib.

TO MAKE UP
Sew on sleeves, placing centre of sleeves to shoulder seams. Join sleeve seams. Sew on buttons. Fold neckband to wrong side and slip stitch in place, then catch down open edges to front bands. With A, embroider eye on each duck.

Sailor Top with Teddy

See Page
29

MATERIALS
Sailor Top 8(9: 10) 50g balls of Rowan Cotton Glace in Navy (A).
1 ball of same in White (B).
Pair each of 2¾mm (No 12/US 2) and 3¼mm (No 10/US 3) knitting needles.
Teddy 1 25g hank of Rowan Lightweight DK in Gold (A).
1 50g ball of Rowan Cotton Glace in each of Navy (B), White (C) and Red (D).
Small amount of Rowan True 4 ply Botany in Blue (E).
Length of Black yarn for embroidery.
Pair each of 2¾mm (No 12/US 2) and 3¼mm (No 10/US 3) knitting needles.
Stuffing.

TENSION
25 sts and 34 rows to 10cm/4in square over st st on 3¼mm (No 10/US 3) needles using Cotton Glace yarn.

ABBREVIATIONS
See page 7.

MEASUREMENTS
Sailor Top

To fit age	2	3	4	years
Actual chest	74	78	83	cm
measurement	29	30¾	32¾	in
Length	40	43	46	cm
	15¾	17	18	in
Sleave seam	24	28	31	cm
	9½	11	12¼	in

Teddy
Approximately 15cm/6in high.

Sailor Top

BACK
With 2¾mm (No 12/US 2) needles and A, cast on 92(98: 104) sts.
K 7 rows.
Change to 3¼mm (No 10/US 3) needles.
Next row (right side) K to end.
Next row K5, p to last 5 sts, k5.
Rep last 2 rows 3 times more.**
Beg with a k row, work in st st across all sts until Back measures 24(25: 26)cm/9½(10: 10¼)in from beg, ending with a p row.
Next row K to end.
Next row P5, k6, p to last 11 sts, k6, p5.
Rep last 2 rows until Back measures 40(43: 46)cm/15¾(17: 18)in from beg, ending with a wrong side row.
Shape Shoulders
Cast off 24(26: 28) sts at beg of next 2 rows. Cast off rem 44(46: 48) sts.

POCKET LINING
With 3¼mm (No 10/US 3) needles and A, cast on 34 sts. Work 13cm/5in in st st, ending with a k row.

FRONT
Work as given for Back to **. Beg with a k row, work in st st across all sts until Front measures 14cm/5½in from beg, ending with a p row.
Place Pocket
Next row K to end.
Next row P29(32: 35), k34, p to end.
Rep last 2 rows 3 times more.
Next row K29(32: 35), cast off next 34 sts, k to end.
Next row P29(32: 35), p across sts of pocket lining, p to end.
Cont in st st until Front measures 24(25:26)cm/9½(10: 10¼)in from beg, ending with a p row.
Next row K to end.
Next row P5, k6, p to last 11 sts, k6, p5.
Rep last 2 rows until Front measures 29(31: 33)cm/11½(12¼ 13)in from beg, ending with a wrong side row.
Shape Neck
Next row Patt 46(49: 52), turn.
Work on this set off sts only. Dec one st at neck edge on every row until 34(39: 44) sts rem, then on every alt row until 24(26: 28) sts rem. Cont straight until Front matches Back to shoulder shaping, ending at side edge. Cast off.

With right side facing, rejoin yarn to rem sts, patt to end. Complete to match first side.

SLEEVES

With 2¾mm (No 12/US 2) needles and A, cast on 38(42: 42) sts.

1st rib row (right side) K2, [p2, k2] to end.

2nd rib row P2, [k2, p2] to end.
Rib 13 rows more.

Next row Rib 4(7: 3), inc in next st, [rib 5(8: 6), inc in next st] to last 3(7: 3) sts, rib to end. 44(46: 48) sts.
Change to 3¼mm (No 10/US 3) needles. Beg with a k row, work in st st, inc one st at each end of 2nd(2nd: 3rd) row until there are 64(56: 92) sts, then on every foll 3rd(3rd: 4th) row until there are 88(96: 100) sts. Cont straight until Sleeve measures 24(28: 31)cm/9½(11: 12¼)in from beg, ending with a wrong side row. Cast off.

COLLAR

With 2¾mm (No 12/US 2) needles and A, cast on 86(92: 98) sts.
K 5 rows.
Change to 3¼mm (No 10/US 3) needles.

Next row (right side) K to end.

Next row K6, p to last 6 sts, k6.
Rep last 2 rows until Collar measures 14(15: 16)cm/5½(6: 6¼)in from beg, ending with a wrong side row.

Next row Patt 33(35: 37), cast off next 20(22: 24) sts, patt to end.
Work on last set of sts only. Patt 1 row. Cast off 3 sts at beg of next row and foll alt row. Dec one st at inside edge on foll right side row and foll 4th row, then on every alt row until 5 sts rem. K 30 rows on rem 5 sts for tie. Cast off.
With wrong side facing, rejoin yarn to rem sts, patt to end. Complete to match first side.

INSET

With 3¼mm (No 10/US 3) needles and B, cast on 3 sts.
Beg with a k row, work in st st and stripes of 2 rows B, 2 rows A, **at the same time**, inc one st at each end of 1st row and every foll 3rd row until there are 25 sts. Work 1 row. With B, k 4 rows. Cast off.

TO MAKE UP

Join shoulder seams. Sew on sleeves, placing centre of sleeves to shoulder seams. Join sleeve seams, then side seams to top of garter st borders. Sew on collar, leaving ties free. Sew inset in place.

Teddy

RIGHT AND LEFT LEGS, BODY, ARMS, HEAD AND EARS

Work as Right and Left Legs, Body, Arms, Head and Ears of Teddy of Fair Isle Ballet Top with Shoes and Teddy (see page 52), but using 2¾mm (No 12/US 2) needles.

TROUSERS

With 3¼mm (No 10/US 3) needles and B, cast on 16 sts.
K 3 rows. Beg with a k row, work 8 rows in st st. Mark each end of last row. Work a further 8 rows. P 3 rows. Cast off purlwise. Make one more. Join leg seams to markers, then join back and front centre seams.

SWEATER

With 3¼mm (No 10/US 3) needles and C, cast on 18 sts for body.
K 4 rows. P 1 row. Cont in st st and stripes of 2 rows D and 4 rows C

throughout, work 9 rows.
Shape Neck

Next row P4, cast off next 10 sts, p to end.

Next row K4, cast on 10 sts, k to end. Work 11 rows. With C, p 3 rows. Cast off purlwise.
With 3¼mm (No 10/US 3) needles, C and right side facing, pick up and k12 sts along side edge of body between first and last D stripe for sleeve. Beg with a p row, cont in st st, work 3 rows C, 2 rows D, 3 rows C. With C, k 3 rows. Cast off. Work other sleeve in same way. Join side and sleeve seams.

SCARF

With 3¼mm (No 10/US 3) needles and E, cast on 36 sts. K 1 row.

Next 2 rows Cast off 4, k to end.
Beg with a k row, work in st st, dec one st at each end of every row until 2 sts rem. Work 2 tog and fasten off.

TO MAKE UP

Fold sides of body to centre and join cast on edge. Gather neck edge, pull up and secure. Join back seam, leaving an opening. Stuff and close opening. Sew head in position. Fold ears in half widthwise and stitch together open edges. Sew ears in place. With Black, embroider nose, mouth and eyes. Attach yarn at seam about 1cm/⅜in down from top of one arm, thread yarn through body at shoulder position, then attach other arm, pull yarn tightly and thread through body again in same place, then attach to first arm again and fasten off. Attach legs at hip position in same way as arms.

Jacket with Sampler Panels

See Page
30

Front motif

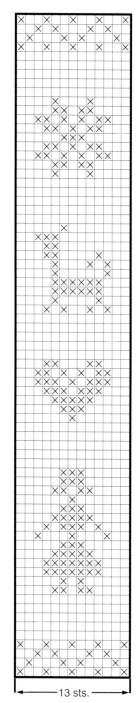

13 sts.

MATERIALS
6(7) 50g balls of Rowan Cotton Glace in Red (A).
1 ball of same in Cream.
Pair each of 3¼mm (No 10/US 3) and 3¾mm (No 9/US 4) knitting needles.
Cable needle.
5 buttons.

MEASUREMENTS

To fit age	6	12	months
Actual chest	56	63	cm
measurement	22	24¾	in
Length	36	40	cm
	14¼	15¾	in
Sleeve seam	18	20	cm
	7	8	in

TENSION
25 sts and 34 rows to 10cm/4in square over st st on 3¼mm (No 10/US 3) needles.

ABBREVIATIONS
C4B = sl next 2 sts onto cable needle and leave at back of work, k2, then k2 from cable needle;
C4F = sl next 2 sts onto cable needle and leave at front of work, k2, then k2 from cable needle.
Also see page 7.

LEFT FRONT
With 3¼mm (No 10/US 3) needles and A, cast on 67(71) sts.
1st row K1, [p1, k1] to end.
This row forms moss st. Work 5 rows more in moss st.
Next row (right side) K to last 4 sts, moss st 4.
Next row Moss st 4, p to end.
Rep last 2 rows until Front measures 11(13)cm/4¼(5)in from beg, ending with a right side row.
Dec row Moss st 4, p5(7), [p2 tog, p1] twice, [p2 tog] twice, * [p2 tog] twice, p3 tog; rep from * 3 times more, [p2 tog] 3 times, [p1, p2 tog] twice, p8(10). 42(46) sts.

Work in patt as follows:
1st row (right side) K8(10), p1, C4B, p1, k13, p1, C4F, p1, k5(7), moss st 4.
2nd row Moss st 4, p5(7), k1, p4, k1, p13, k1, p4, k1, p8(10).
3rd row K8(10), p1, k4, p1, k13, p1, k4, p1, k5(7), moss st 4.
4th row As 2nd row.
These 4 rows form patt. Patt 38(40) rows.
Shape Armhole
Cast off 3 sts at beg of next row. Work 1 row. Dec one st at armhole edge on next 3 rows. 36(40) sts. Patt 26(29) rows.
Keeping the 4 sts at front edge in moss st and remainder in st st, work

Back motif

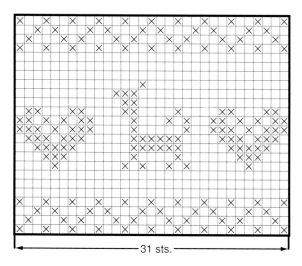

31 sts.

Border pattern

←Rep→
6 sts.

edge
st.

4(5) rows, dec 2 sts over each cable on first row. 32(36) sts.

Shape Neck
Cast off 8 sts at beg of next row and 4(5) sts at beg of foll alt row. Dec one st at neck edge on next 3 rows. 17(20) sts. Work 3 rows.

Shape Shoulder
Cast off 6(7) sts at beg of next row and foll alt row. Work 1 row. Cast off rem 5(6) sts.
Mark front edge to indicate position of 5 buttons: first one 7(9)cm/2¾(3½)in from lower edge, last one 1cm/⅜in below neck shaping and rem 3 evenly spaced between.

RIGHT FRONT
With 3¼mm (No 10/US 3) needles and A, cast on 67(71) sts.
Work 6 rows in moss st as given for Left Front.
Next row (right side) Moss st 4, k to end.
Next row P to last 4 sts, moss st 4.
Rep last 2 rows until Front measures 7(9)cm/2¾(3⅝)in from beg, ending with a wrong side row.
Buttonhole row K1, p1, yrn, p2 tog, patt to end.
Complete as given for Left Front, making buttonholes at markers, reversing shapings and working dec row and patt as follows:
Dec row P8(10), [p2 tog, p1] twice, [p2 tog] 3 times, * p3 tog, [p2 tog] twice; rep from * 3 times more, [p2 tog] twice, [p1, p2 tog] twice, p5(7), moss st 4. 42(46) sts.
1st row (right side) Moss st 4, k5(7), p1, C4B, p1, k13, p1, C4F, p1, k8(10).
2nd row P8(10), k1, p4, k1, p13, k1, p4, k1, p5(7), moss st 4.
3rd row Moss st 4, k5(7), p1, k4, p1, k13, p1, k4, p1, k8(10).
4th row As 2nd row.

BACK
With 3¼mm (No 10/US 3) needles and A, cast on 113(121) sts.
Work 6 rows in moss st as given for Left Front.
Beg with a k row, work in st st until Back matches Left Front to armhole shaping, ending with a p row.
Shape Armholes
Cast off 3 sts at beg of next 2 rows.

Swiss Darning
Bring needle out to front at base of stitch to be covered. Insert needle under the base of stitch above then back at base. Emerge at base of next stitch to be covered

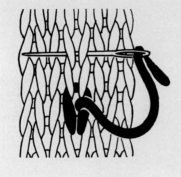

Dec one st at each end of next 3 rows. 101(109) sts. Work 1(4) rows.
Dec row Work 14(18), work 3 tog, *[work 2 tog] twice, work 3 tog; rep from * 9 times more, work 14(18). 59(67) sts.
Cont straight until Back matches Left Front to shoulder shaping, ending with a p row.
Shape Shoulders
Cast off 6(7) sts at beg of next 4 rows and 5(6) sts at beg of foll 2 rows.
Cast off rem 25(27) sts.

SLEEVES
With 3¼mm (No 10/US 3) needles and A, cast on 37(43) sts.
Work 5 rows in moss st as given for Left Front.
Next row Moss st 1(4), work twice in next st, [moss st 2, work twice in next st] 11 times, moss st 2(5). 49(55) sts.
Beg with a k row, work in st st, inc one st at each end of 9th row and every foll 4th row until there are 67(75) sts.
Cont straight until Sleeve measures 18(20)cm/7(8)in from beg, ending with a p row.
Shape Top
Cast off 3 sts at beg of next 2 rows.
Dec one st at each end of next row and foll alt row. Work 1 row. Cast off rem 57(65) sts.

COLLAR
Join shoulder seams.
With 3¼mm (No 10/US 3) needles, right side facing, A and beg at centre of buttonhole band, pick up and k21(23) sts up right front neck, 25(27) sts across back neck and k21(23) sts down left front neck to centre of button band. 67(73) sts.
Next row K1, p1, k to last 2 sts, p1, k1.
Next row K1, p1, k1, p to last 3 sts, k1, p1, k1.
Rep last 2 rows 3 times more.
Change to 3¾mm (No 9/US 4) needles and work 8 rows.
Work 4 rows in moss st across all sts.
Cast off loosely in moss st.

TO MAKE UP
With Cream, swiss darn (see diagram) front motifs between cables, beg above dec row, reversing reindeer motif on one front and working 1 row more between each motif on **2nd size** only.
Beg above dec row at centre of back yoke, swiss darn back motif with Cream. Swiss darn with Cream border patt on sleeves and collar, beg 2 rows above moss st.
Join side and sleeve seams. Sew in sleeves. Sew on buttons.

Toy Sweater

See Page
31

MATERIALS
5 50g balls of Rowan Designer DK Wool in Dark Green (A).
1 ball of same in each of Red, Purple, Dark Blue, Pale Blue, Light Green, Beige, Brown and Bright Green.
Pair each of 3¼mm (No 10/US 3) and 4mm (No 8/US 6) knitting needles.

MEASUREMENTS

To fit age	2-4	years
Actual chest	80	cm
measurement	31½	in
Length	42	cm
	16½	in
Sleeve seam	26	cm
	10¼	in

TENSION
24 sts and 32 rows to 10cm/4in square over st st on 4mm (No 8/US 6) needles.

ABBREVIATIONS
See page 7.

NOTE
Read charts from right to left on right side (k) rows and from left to right on wrong side (p) rows. When working in pattern from chart, use separate lengths of contrast colours for each coloured area and twist yarns together on wrong side at joins to avoid holes.

Chart 2

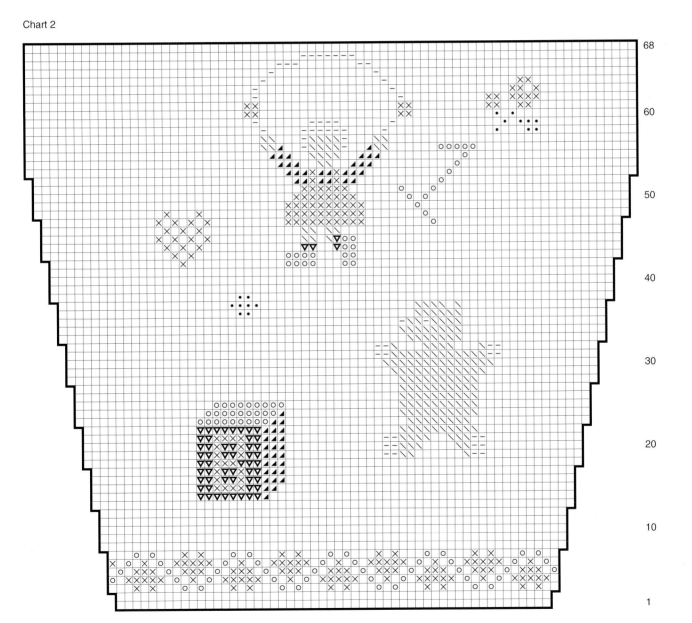

Chart 1

Key

☐ = Dark Green (A)

☒ = Red

☉ = Purple

◪ = Dark Blue

▽ = Pale Blue

◮ = Light Green

⊠ = Beige

⊟ = Brown

⊡ = Bright Green

BACK

With 4mm (No 8/US 6) needles and A, cast on 94 sts.
Beg with a k row, work 4 rows in st st.

1st rib row (right side) K2, [p2, k2] to end.
2nd rib row P2, [k2, p2] to end.
Rib a further 8 rows, inc 2 sts evenly across last row. 96 sts.
Beg with a k row, work in st st and patt from chart 1 until 122nd row of chart 1 has been worked.
Shape Shoulders
Next row With A, cast off 29, k to last 29 sts, cast off these sts.
Leave rem 38 sts on a holder.

FRONT

Work as given for Back until 104th row of chart 1 has been worked.
Shape Neck
Next row Patt 36, turn.
Work on this set of sts only. Cont in patt from chart, dec one st at neck edge on next 7 rows. 29 sts. Patt 10 rows straight. With A, cast off.
With right side facing, slip centre 24 sts onto a holder, rejoin yarn to rem sts, patt to end. Complete to match first side.

SLEEVES

With 3¼mm (No 10/US 3) needles and A, cast on 54 sts.
Beg with a k row, work 4 rows in st st.
Work 14 rows in rib as given for Back.

Change to 4mm (No 8/US 6) needles.
Beg with a k row, work in st st and patt from chart 2, inc one st at each end of 3rd row and every foll 5th row until there are 76 sts. Cont straight until 68th row of chart 2 has been worked. Cast off.

NECKBAND

Join right shoulder seam.
With 4mm (No 8/US 6) needles, A and right side facing, pick up and k16 sts down left front neck, k centre front sts, pick up and k16 sts up right front neck, k back neck sts. 94 sts. Beg with a 2nd row, work 7 rows in rib as given for Back. Beg with a k row, work 4 rows in st st. Cast off loosely.

TO MAKE UP

Join left shoulder and neckband seam, reversing seam on st st section of neckband. Sew on sleeves, placing centre of sleeves to shoulder seams. Join side and sleeve seams, reversing seam on st st sections at lower edges. With A, embroider eye on each rocking horse and face features and button on each rabbit. Embroider mouth with Red on each boy and girl and bow with Purple on girl's hair.

Coat with Contrast Lining

See Page
32

MATERIALS
7 50g balls of Rowan Designer DK Wool in each of Green (A) and Cream (B).
Pair of 4½mm (No 7/US 7) knitting needles.
4 buttons.

TENSION
22 sts and 30 rows to 10cm/4in square over st st on 4½mm (No 7/US 7) needles.

MEASUREMENTS

To fit age	2-4 years
Actual chest	82 cm
measurement	32¼ in
Length	41 cm
	16 in
Sleeve seam	20 cm
(with cuff turned back)	8 in

ABBREVIATIONS
See page 7.

Outer Layer

POCKET LININGS (make 2)
With 4½mm (No 7/US 7) needles and B, cast on 22 sts.
Beg with a k row, work 23 rows in st st. Leave these sts on a holder.

BACK AND FRONTS
Worked in one piece to armholes.
With 4½mm (No 7/US 7) needles and A, cast on 195 sts.
Beg with a k row, work 38 rows in st st.
Place Pockets
Next row K18, cast off next 22 sts, k to last 40 sts, cast off next 22 sts, k to end.

Next row P18, p across sts of first pocket lining, p to last 18 sts, p across sts of second pocket lining, p to end.
Work 30 rows.
Right Front
Next row K52, turn.
Work 37 rows on this set of sts only.
Shape Neck
Cast off 8 sts at beg of next row and foll alt row. Dec one st at neck edge on next 5 rows. 31 sts. Work 6 rows straight. Leave these sts on a holder.
Back
With right side facing, rejoin yarn to rem sts on needle and k91, turn. Work 51 rows on this set of sts only. Leave these sts on a spare needle.
Left Front
With right side facing, rejoin yarn to rem 52 sts on needle and work 37 rows on these sts.
Shape Neck
Cast off 8 sts at beg of next row and foll alt row. Dec one st at neck edge on

next 5 rows. 31 sts. Work 7 rows straight.

Shoulders

Next row With right sides of fronts and back together, cast off tog left shoulder sts, slip next 29 sts onto a holder for back neck, cast off tog right shoulder sts.

SLEEVES

With 4½mm (No 7/US 7) needles and A, cast on 57 sts.

Work in st st, inc one st at each end of 15th row and 9 foll 6th rows. 77 sts. Work 7 rows straight. Cast off.

HOOD

With 4½mm (No 7/US 7) needles, A and omitting first 8 cast off sts at neck edge, pick up and k20 sts up right front neck, k back neck sts, pick up and k20 sts down left front neck, omitting first 8 cast off sts. 69 sts.

Next row P1, [p twice in next st, p1] to end. 103 sts.

Beg with a k row, work 2 rows in st st.

Next row K51, m1, k1, m1, k51.

Work 3 rows straight.

Next row K52, m1, k1, m1, k52.

Cont in this way, inc 2 sts as set at centre back on 3 foll 4th rows. 113 sts. Work 51 rows straight dec one st at centre of last row. Divide sts equally onto 2 needles, pointing needles in same direction and with right side inside, cast off tog hood sts.

TO MAKE UP

Sew in sleeves, placing centre of sleeves to shoulder seams. Join sleeve seams. Catch down pocket linings.

Lining

BACK AND FRONTS

Work in one piece to armholes.

With 4½mm (No 7/US 7) needles and B, cast on 188 sts.

Beg with a k row, work 66 rows in st st.

Right Front

Next row K50, turn.

Work 35 rows on this set of sts only.

Shape Neck

Cast off 8 sts at beg of next row and 7 sts at beg of foll alt row. Dec one st at neck edge on next 5 rows. 30 sts. Work 6 rows straight. Leave these sts on a holder.

Back

With right side facing, rejoin yarn to rem sts on needle and k88, turn. Work 49 rows on this set of sts only. Leave these sts on a spare needle.

Left Front

With right side facing, rejoin yarn to rem 50 sts on needle and work 35 rows on these sts.

Shape Neck

Cast off 8 sts at beg of next row and 7 sts at beg of foll alt row. Dec one st at neck edge on next 5 rows. 30 sts. Work 7 rows straight.

Shoulders

Next row With right sides of fronts and back together, cast off tog left shoulder sts, slip next 28 sts onto a holder for back neck, cast off tog right shoulder sts.

SLEEVES

With 4½mm (No 7/US 7) needles and B, cast on 59 sts.

Work in st st, dec one st at each end of 17th row. Cont in st st, inc one st at each end of 8 foll 7th rows. 73 sts. Work 7 rows straight. Cast off.

HOOD

With 4½mm (No 7/US 7) needles and B and omitting first 8 cast off sts at neck edge, pick up and k19 sts up right front neck, k back neck sts, pick up and k19 sts down left front neck, omitting first 8 cast off sts. 66 sts.

Next row [P1, p twice in next st] to end. 99 sts.

Beg with a k row, work 2 rows in st st.

Next row K49, m1, k1, m1, k49.

Work 3 rows straight.

Next row K50, m1, k1, m1, k50.

Cont in this way, inc 2 sts as set at centre back on 3 foll 4th rows. 109 sts. Work 46 rows straight dec one st at centre of last row. Divide sts equally onto 2 needles, pointing needles in same direction and with right side inside, cast off tog hood sts.

TO MAKE UP

Sew on sleeves, placing centre of sleeves to shoulder seams. Join sleeve seams. Turn lining inside out. Insert lining into outer layer and catch together on wrong side in few places at shoulders and top of hood. Join together all open edges. Mark one front edge to indicate position of buttonholes: first one 1cm/½in below neck edge, last one 10cm/4in up from lower edge and rem 2 evenly spaced between. Push large knitting needle through both thicknesses at markers thus forming holes. Sew on buttons. Turn back cuffs.

Moss Stitch and Cable Waistcoat

See Page 33

MATERIALS
5 50g balls of Rowan Cotton Glace.
Pair each of 2¾mm (No 12/US 2) and
3¼mm (No 10/US 3) knitting needles.
Cable needle.
3 buttons.

MEASUREMENTS
To fit age	1–2	years
Actual chest	61	cm
measurement	24	in
Length	29	cm
	11½	in

BACK
With 3¼mm (No 10/US 3) needles cast
on 90 sts.
1st row (right side) K1, p1, k1, *k1, p1,
C4B, C4F, [p1, k1] 4 times; rep from * 3
times more, k1, p1, C4B, C4F, [p1, k1]
twice, p1.
2nd row P1, k1, p1, *[p1, k1] 4 times,
p2, [k1, p1] 4 times; rep from * 3 times
more, [p1, k1] 4 times, p2, [k1, p1]
twice, k1.
3rd row K1, p1, k1, *[k1, p1] 4 times,
k2, [p1, k1] 4 times; rep from * 3 times
more, [k1, p1] 4 times, k2, [p1, k1]
twice, p1.
4th and 5th rows As 2nd and 3rd rows.
6th row As 2nd row.
7th row K1, p1, k1, *[k1, p1] twice, k3,
p1, k2, [p1, k1] 4 times; rep from * 3
times more, [k1, p1] twice, k3, p1, k2,
[p1, k1] twice, p1.
8th row P1, k1, p1, *[p1, k1] twice, p3,
k1, p2, [k1, p1] 4 times; rep from * 3
times more, [p1, k1] twice, p3, k1, p2,
[k1, p1] twice, k1.
These 8 rows form patt. Cont in patt
until Back measures 13cm/5¼in from
beg, ending with a wrong side row.
Shape Armholes
Keeping patt correct, cast off 6 sts at
beg of next 2 rows. Dec one st at
armhole edge on next 11 rows. 56 sts.
Cont straight until Back measures
27cm/10¾in from beg, ending with a
wrong side row.
Shape Shoulder and Neck
Next row Patt 17, turn.
Work on this set of sts only. Cast off 4
sts at beg of next row and 6 sts at beg
of foll row. Patt 1 row. Cast off rem sts.
With right side facing, rejoin yarn to
rem sts, cast off centre 22 sts, patt to
end. Patt 1 row. Cast off 4 sts at beg of
next row and 6 sts at beg of foll row.

TENSION
26 sts and 40 rows to 10cm/4in square
over moss stitch on 3¼mm (No 10/US 3)
needles.

ABBREVIATIONS
C4B = sl next 3 sts onto cable needle
and leave at back of work, k1, then p1,
k1, p1 from cable needle;
C4F = sl next st onto cable needle and
leave at front of work, k1, p1, k1, then k1
from cable needle.
Also see page 7.

Work 1 row. Cast off rem sts.

LEFT FRONT
With 3¼mm (No 10/US 3) needles cast
on 3 sts.
P 1 row.
1st row (right side) Cast on 3, [k2, p1]
twice.
2nd row K1, p1, k1, p3.
3rd row Cast on 3, C4B, C4F, [p1, k1]
in last st.
4th row [P1, k1] 4 times, p2.
5th row Cast on 3, k1, [k1, p1] 4 times,
k2, p1, [k1, p1] in last st.
6th row P1, [p1, k1] 4 times, p2, k1,
p1, k1.
7th row Cast on 2, k1, p1, k1, [k1, p1]
4 times, k2, p1, k1, [p1, k1] in last st.
8th row K1, p1, [p1, k1] 4 times, p2,
[k1, p1] twice, k1.
9th row Cast on 3, [p1, k1] 3 times,
[k1, p1] twice, k3, p1, k2, p1, k1, p1,
[k1, p1] in last st.
10th row P1, k1, p1, [p1, k1] twice, p3,
k1, p2, [k1, p1] 4 times.
Keeping patt correct, cont to cast on 3
sts at beg of next row and 4 foll alt
rows, **at the same time,** inc one st at
end of next row and 4 foll alt rows. 41
sts. Cont in patt until side edge of Front
matches Back to armhole shaping,
ending with a wrong side row.
Shape Armhole and Neck
Next row Cast off 6, patt to last 4 sts,
work 2 tog, patt 2.
Patt 1 row. Dec one st at armhole edge
on next 11 rows, **at the same time,** dec
one st at neck edge as before on next
row and 4 foll alt rows. 18 sts. Cont to
dec at neck edge only on 2nd row and
4 foll 4th rows. 13 sts. Work straight
until Front matches Back to shoulder
shaping, ending at armhole edge.
Shape Shoulder

Cast off 6 sts at beg of next row. Patt 1
row. Cast off rem sts.

RIGHT FRONT
With 3¼mm (No 10/US 3) needles cast
on 3 sts.
P 1 row.
1st row P1, k1, p1.
2nd row Cast on 3, [p2, k1] twice.
3rd row [K1, p1] in first st, C4B, k1.
4th row Cast on 3, [p1, k1] 3 times,
p2, k1, p1.
5th row K twice in first st, p1, [k1, p1]
3 times, k2.
6th row Cast on 3, p1, [p1, k1] 4
times, p2, k1, p2.
7th row [P1, k1] in first st, [k1, p1] 4
times, k2, p1, k1, p1.
8th row Cast on 2, p1, k1, p1, [p1, k1]
4 times, p2, [k1, p1] twice.
9th row [K1, p1] in first st, k1, [k1, p1]
twice, k3, p1, k2, [p1, k1] twice, p1.
10th row Cast on 3, [k1, p1] 3 times,
[p1, k1] twice, p3, k1, p2, k1, [p1, k1]
twice.
Keeping patt correct, cont to inc one st
at beg of next row and 4 foll alt rows,
at the same time, cast on 3 sts at beg
of 5 foll alt rows. 41 sts. Cont in patt
until side edge of Front matches Back
to armhole shaping, ending with a
wrong side row.
Shape Armhole and Neck
Next row Patt 2, work 2 tog, patt to end.
Next row Cast off 6 sts at beg of next
row.
Complete to match Left Front.

ARMBANDS (make 2)
Join shoulder seams.
With 2¾mm (No 12/US 2) needles cast
on 10 sts.
Work in k1, p1 rib until band, when
slightly stretched, fits around armhole
edge. Cast off in rib. Sew band in
place.

LEFT LOWER EDGE BAND,
BUTTON BAND AND LAPEL
Join side and armband seams.
With 2¾mm (No 12/US 2) needles cast
on 10 sts.
Work in p1, k1 rib until band, when
slightly stretched, fits lower edge from
centre of back to point on Left Front,
ending at outside edge.
** **Next 2 rows** Rib 7, yb, sl 1, yf, turn,
sl 1, rib to end.
Next 2 rows Rib 5, yb, sl 1, yf, turn,
sl 1, rib to end.
Next 2 rows Rib 3, yb, sl 1, yf, turn, sl

1, rib to end.
Rib 2 rows.
Next 2 rows Rib 3, yb, sl 1, yf, turn, sl 1, rib to end.
Next 2 rows Rib 5, yb, sl 1, yf, turn, sl 1, rib to end.
Next 2 rows Rib 7, yb, sl 1, yf, turn, sl 1, rib to end. **
Cont in rib across all sts until band fits lower edge of front from point to corner, ending at outside edge. Rep from ** to **. Cont in rib until band fits front edge to beg of neck shaping, ending at inside edge.

Shape Lapel
Inc one st at beg of next row and every foll alt row until there are 21 sts, then on 3 foll 4th rows. 24 sts. Rib 2 rows. Cast off in rib.
Mark band to indicate position of 3 buttons: first one 2 rows after corner shaping, last one 2 rows below lapel shaping and rem one evenly spaced between.

RIGHT LOWER EDGE BAND, BUTTONHOLE BAND
With 2¾mm (No 12/US 2) needles cast on 10 sts.
Work in k1, p1 rib until band, when slightly stretched, fits lower edge from centre of back to point on Right Front, ending at outside edge.
***Next 2 rows** Rib 7, yf, sl 1, yb, turn, sl 1, rib to end.
Next 2 rows Rib 5, yf, sl 1, yb, turn, sl 1, rib to end.
Next 2 rows Rib 3, yf, sl 1, yb, turn, sl 1, rib to end.
Rib 2 rows.
Next 2 rows Rib 3, yf, sl 1, yb, turn, sl 1, rib to end.
Next 2 rows Rib 5, yf, sl 1, yb, turn, sl 1, rib to end.
Next 2 rows Rib 7, yf, sl 1, yb, turn, sl 1, rib to end. ***
Cont in rib across all sts until band fits lower edge of front from point to corner, ending at outside edge. Rep from *** to ***. Rib 2 rows.
Buttonhole row (right side) Rib 4, yrn, p2 tog, rib to end.

Complete to match Left Lower Edge Band, Button Band and Lapel, making buttonholes to match markers.

COLLAR
With 2¾mm (No 12/US 2) needles, wrong side facing and beginning 22 rows below shoulder seam, pick up and k19 sts up left front neck, 6 sts down left back neck, 23 sts across centre back, k6 sts up right back neck and 19 sts down right front neck, ending 22 rows below shoulder seam. 73 sts.
1st rib row K1, [p1, k1] to end.
This row sets rib.
Next 2 rows Rib to last 16 sts, turn.
Next 2 rows Rib to last 12 sts, turn.
Cont in this way, working 4 sts more at end of next 6 rows. Work a further 5cm/2in in rib. Cast off loosely in rib.

TO MAKE UP
Sew front bands with lapels in place and join bands at centre back. Join lapel to collar for 2cm/½in from pick up row. Sew on buttons.

Cardigan with Lace Edging

See Page 35

MATERIALS
6 50g balls of Rowan Cotton Glace in Red (A).
1 ball of same in each of Blue, White and Yellow.
Pair each of 2¾mm (No 12/US 2) and 3¼mm (No 10/US 3) knitting needles.
Cable needle.
4 buttons.

MEASUREMENTS

To fit age	2–3	years
Actual chest	74	cm
measurement	29	in
Length	32	cm
	12½	in
Sleeve seam	23	cm
	9	in

TENSION
25 sts and 34 rows to 10cm/4in square over st st on 3¼mm (No 10/US 3) needles.

ABBREVIATIONS
C4F = sl next 2 sts onto cable needle and leave at front of work, k2, then k2 from cable needle.
Also see page 7.

NOTE
When working in pattern from chart, use separate lengths of contrast colours for each coloured area and twist yarns together on wrong side at joins to avoid holes.

CABLE PANEL
Worked over 29 sts.
1st row (right side) P2, k4, p2, k13, p2, k4, p2.
2nd row K2, p4, k2, p6, k1, p6, k2, p4, k2.
3rd row P2, C4F, p2, k5, p1, k1, p1, k5, p2, C4F, p2.
4th row [K2, p4] twice, k1, [p1, k1] twice, [p4, k2] twice.
5th row P2, k4, p2, k3, p1, [k1, p1] 3 times, k3, p2, k4, p2.
6th row K2, p4, k2, p2, k1, [p1, k1] 4 times, p2, k2, p4, k2.

7th row P2, C4F, p2, k1, [p1, k1] 6 times, p2, C4F, p2.
8th row As 6th row.
9th row As 5th row.
10th row As 4th row.
11th row As 3rd row.
12th row As 2nd row.
These 12 rows form patt.

BACK
With 3¼mm (No 10/US 3) needles and A, cast on 93 sts.
1st row (right side) Reading chart from right to left, k 1st to 49th sts of chart, then reading chart from left to right, k 44th to 1st sts.
2nd row Reading chart from right to left, p 1st to 49th sts, then reading chart from left to right, p 44th to 1st sts.
Work a further 17 rows as set. Cont in A only.
Next row P8, [m1, p7] 12 times, p1. 105 sts.
Work in cable patt as follows:
1st row K1, [p1, k1] 5 times, work 1st row of cable panel, k1, [p1, k1] 12 times, work 1st row of cable panel, k1, [p1, k1] 5 times.

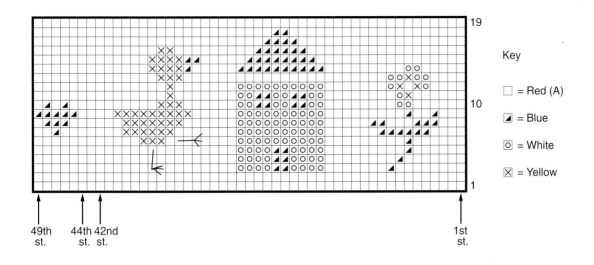

49th
st.

44th
st.

42nd
st.

1st
st.

This row sets position of panels and forms moss st at each side of panels. Cont in cable patt until Back measures 29cm/11½in from beg, ending with a wrong side row.

Shape Shoulders

Cast off 8 sts at beg of next 8 rows. Leave rem 41 sts on a holder.

LEFT FRONT

With 3¼mm (No 10/US 3) needles and A, cast on 42 sts.

1st row (right side) Reading chart from right to left, k 1st to 42nd sts of chart.

2nd row Reading chart from left to right, p 42nd to 1st sts.

Work a further 17 rows as set. Cont in A only.

Next row P3, [m1, p5] 7 times, m1, p4. 50 sts.

Work in cable patt as follows:

1st row K1, [p1, k1] 5 times, work 1st row of cable panel, [k1, p1] 5 times.

2nd row [P1, k1] 5 times, work 2nd row of cable panel, k1, [p1, k1] 5 times.

These 2 rows set position of panel and form moss st at each side of panel.

Cont in cable patt until Front measures 14cm/5½in from beg, ending with a wrong side row.

Shape Neck

Keeping patt correct, dec one st at neck edge on next row and 12 foll alt rows, then on every foll 3rd row until 32 sts rem. Cont straight until Front matches Back to shoulder shaping, ending at side edge.

Shape Shoulder

Cast off 8 sts at beg of next row and 2 foll

alt rows. Work 1 row. Cast off rem 8 sts.

RIGHT FRONT

With 3¼mm (No 10/US 3) needles and A, cast on 42 sts.

1st row (right side) Reading chart from left to right, k 42nd to 1st sts.

2nd row Reading chart from right to left, p 1st to 42nd sts.

Work a further 17 rows as set. Cont in A only.

Next row P4, [m1, p5] 7 times, m1, p3. 50 sts.

Work in cable patt as follows:

1st row [P1, k1] 5 times, work 1st row of cable panel, k1, [p1, k1] 5 times.

2nd row K1, [p1, k1] 5 times, work 2nd row of cable panel, [k1, p1] 5 times.

These 2 rows set position of panel and form moss st at each side of panel.

Complete to match Left Front.

SLEEVES

With 3¼mm (No 10/US 3) needles and A, cast on 59 sts.

1st row K1, [p1, k1] 7 times, work 1st row of cable panel, k1, [p1, k1] 7 times. This row sets position of panel and forms moss st at each side of panel.

Cont in cable patt, inc one st at each end of 2nd row and every foll 5th row until there are 83 sts, working inc sts into moss st. Cont straight until Sleeve measures 20cm/8in from beg, ending with a wrong side row. Cast off.

FRONT BAND

Join shoulder seams.

With 2¾mm (No 12/US 2) needles, A

and right side facing, pick up and k38 sts along straight right front edge to beg of neck shaping, 50 sts along shaped edge to shoulder, k back neck sts, pick up and k50 sts along shaped edge of left front to beg of neck shaping and 38 sts down straight edge to cast on edge. 217 sts.

1st rib row P1, [k1, p1] to end.

2nd rib row K1, [p1, k1] to end.

Buttonhole row Rib to last 38 sts, [k2 tog, yf, rib 9] 3 times, k2 tog, yf, rib 3. Rib 2 rows. Cast off in rib.

SLEEVE EDGINGS (make 2)

With 2¾mm (No 12/US 2) needles and A, cast on 4 sts.

K 1 row.

1st row (right side) K2, yf, k2.

2nd row and 2 foll alt rows Sl 1, k to end.

3rd row K3, yf, k2.

5th row K2, yf, k2 tog, yf, k2.

7th row K3, yf, k2 tog, yf, k2.

8th row Cast off 4, k to end.

These 8 rows form patt. Cont in patt until edging, when slightly stretched, fits along lower edge of sleeve, ending with 8th row. Cast off.

TO MAKE UP

Sew on sleeve edgings. Placing centre of sleeves to shoulder seams, sew on sleeves. Join side and sleeve seams. Make edging as sleeve edgings to fit lower edge of cardigan and sew in place. Sew on buttons. Embroider legs and feet with Blue and eye with White on each chick.

Ducks and Boats Sweater

See Page
34

MATERIALS

4 50g balls of Rowan Designer DK Wool in Green (A).
1 ball of same in each of Blue, Cream, Red, Navy, Jade and Yellow.
Pair of 4mm (No 8/US 6) knitting needles.

MEASUREMENTS

To fit age	2-3	years
Actual chest	78	cm
measurement	30¾	in
Length	36	cm
	14	in
Sleeve seam	20	cm
	8	in

TENSION

24 sts and 32 rows to 10cm/4in square over st st on 4mm (No 8/US 6) needles.

ABBREVIATIONS

See page 7.

NOTE

Read chart from right to left on right side (k) rows and from left to right on wrong side (p) rows. Use separate lengths of contrast colours for each coloured area of duck and boat motifs of pattern and twist yarns together on wrong side at joins to avoid holes. When working Fair Isle bands of pattern, strand yarn not in use loosely across wrong side over no more than 5 sts at the time to keep fabric elastic.

BACK AND FRONT (alike)

With 4mm (No 8/US 6) needles and A, cast on 98 sts.
Beg with a k row, work 4 rows in st st. Cont in st st and work in patt from chart as follows: work 1st to 52nd rows, 15th to 41st rows, then 3rd to 13th rows.
Shape Neck
Next row With A, k34, turn.
Work on this set of sts only.
Next row With A, p2 tog, p to end.
Next row K 1A, [1Navy, 1A] to last 2 sts, with Navy, k2 tog.
Next row With Navy, p2 tog, [p 1A, 1Navy] to end.
Shape Shoulder
Cont in A only.
Next row Cast off 15, k to last 2 sts, k2 tog.
Next row P2 tog, p to end.
Cast off rem 14 sts.
With right side facing, slip centre 30 sts onto a holder, join A to rem sts and k to end. Work as given for first side, reversing shapings.

SLEEVES

With 4mm (No 8/US 6) needles and A, cast on 50 sts.
Beg with a k row, work 4 rows in st st. Cont in st st and work 1st to 52nd rows of patt from chart, **at the same time**, inc and work into patt one st at each end of 1st row, 6 foll 3rd rows and 7 foll 4th rows. 78 sts. Cast off.

NECKBAND

Join right shoulder seam.
With 4mm (No 8/US 6) needles, A and right side facing, pick up and k7 sts down left front neck, k centre front sts, pick up and k7 sts up right front neck, 7 sts down right back neck, k centre back sts, pick up and k7 sts up left back neck. 88 sts. Beg with a p row, work 7 rows in st st. Cast off loosely.

TO MAKE UP

Join left shoulder and neckband seam, reversing seam on last 4 rows of neckband. Sew on sleeves, placing centre of sleeves to shoulder seams. Join side and sleeve seams.

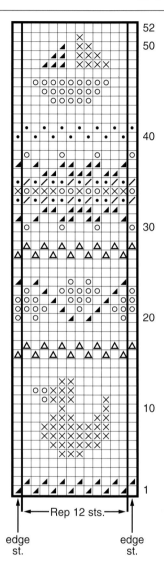

Rep 12 sts.

edge st.   edge st.

□ = Green (A)

◪ = Blue

☒ = Cream

◎ = Red

▲ = Navy

⊡ = Jade

◫ = Yellow

Cable Jacket and Beret

See Page
36

MATERIALS

Jacket 4 50g hanks of Rowan DK Tweed.
Pair each of 3¼mm (No 10/US 3) and 4mm (No 8/US 6) knitting needles.
Cable needle.
7 buttons.
Beret 1 50g hank of Rowan DK Tweed.
Pair each of 3¼mm (No 10/US 3) and 4mm (No 8/US 6) knitting needles.

TENSION

24 sts and 30 rows to 10cm/4in square over cable pattern on 4mm (No 8/US 6) needles.

MEASUREMENTS

To fit age	12–18	months
Actual chest	60	cm
measurement	23½	in
Length	30	cm
	11¾	in
Sleeve seam	20	cm
	8	in

ABBREVIATIONS

C4B = sl next 3 sts onto cable needle and leave at back of work, k1, then p1, k1, p1 from cable needle;
C4F = sl next st onto cable needle and leave at front of work, k1, p1, k1, then k1 from cable needle.
Also see page 7.

Jacket

BACK

With 3¼mm (No 10/US 3) needles cast on 71 sts.
1st row K1, [p1, k1] to end.
The last row forms moss st. Moss st 3 rows more, inc one st at centre of last row. 72 sts.
Change to 4mm (No 8/US 6) needles.
1st row (right side) P2, *C4B, C4F, p2; rep from * to end.
2nd row and 2 foll alt rows K2, *[p1, k1] 3 times, p2, k2; rep from * to end.
3rd row P2, *[k1, p1] 3 times, k2, p2; rep from * to end.
5th row As 3rd row.
7th row P2, *k1, p1, k3, p1, k2, p2; rep from * to end.
8th row K2, *p1, k1, p3, k1, p2, k2; rep from * to end.
These 8 rows form patt. Patt 18 rows more.
Change to 3¼mm (No 10/US 3) needles.
Work 8 rows in k1, p1 rib.
Change to 4mm (No 8/US 6) needles.
Beg with 3rd row, work in patt until Back measures 30cm/11¾in from beg, ending with a wrong side row.
Shape Shoulders
Cast off 11 sts at beg of next 4 rows.
Leave rem 28 sts on a holder.

LEFT FRONT

With 3¼mm (No 10/US 3) needles cast on 37 sts.
Work 4 rows in moss st as given for Back.
Change to 4mm (No 8/US 6) needles.
Keeping 5 sts at front edge in moss st and remainder in patt as given for Back, patt 26 rows.
Change to 3¼mm (No 10/US 3) needles.

1st rib row K1, [p1, k1] to end.
2nd rib row P1, [k1, p1] to end.
Rep last 2 rows 3 times.
Change to 4mm (No 8/US 6) needles.
Work in patt until Front measures 25cm/10in from beg, ending at front edge.
Shape Neck
Next row Patt 5 and slip these 5 sts onto a safety pin, patt to end.
Keeping patt correct, dec one st at neck edge on every row until 22 sts rem. Cont straight until Front matches Back to shoulder shaping, ending at side edge.
Shape Shoulder
Cast off 11 sts at beg of next row. Patt 1 row. Cast off rem 11 sts.
Mark front edge to indicate position of 5 buttons: first one 2 rows up from lower edge, last one 1cm/½in down from neck edge and rem 3 evenly spaced between.

RIGHT FRONT

With 3¼mm (No 10/US 3) needles cast on 37 sts.
Work 2 rows in moss st as given for Back.
Buttonhole row (right side)
K1, p1, yrn, p2 tog, patt to end.
Complete as given for Left Front, working buttonholes to match markers.

SLEEVES

With 3¼mm (No 10/US 3) needles cast on 42 sts.
Work 10 rows in k1, p1 rib.
Change to 4mm (No 8/US 6) needles.
Work in patt as given for Back, inc one st at each end of next row and every foll 5th row until there are 62 sts,

working inc sts into patt. Cont straight until Sleeve measures 20cm/8in from beg, ending with a wrong side row.
Cast off.

COLLAR

Join shoulder seams.
With 3¼mm (No 10/US 3) needles and right side facing, slip 5 sts from right front safety pin onto needle, pick up and k15 sts up right front neck, k back neck sts inc one st, pick up and k15 sts down left front neck, moss st 5 across sts on safety pin. 69 sts. Moss st 1 row.
Next 2 rows Moss st to last 16 sts, turn.
Next 2 rows Moss st to last 12 sts, turn.
Next 2 rows Moss st to last 8 sts, turn.
Next 2 rows Moss st to last 4 sts, turn.
Next row Moss st to end.
Cast off 4 sts at beg of next 2 rows. 61 sts. Moss st 18 rows. Cast off loosely in moss st.

FLAPS (make 2)

With 3¼mm (No 10/US 3) needles cast on 17 sts. Work 10 rows in moss st as given for Back. Dec one st at each end of next row and foll alt row, then at each end of next 3 rows. Cast off.

TO MAKE UP

Sew on sleeves, placing centre of sleeves to shoulder seams. Join side and sleeve seams. Sew on flaps and buttons.

Beret

With 3¼mm (No 10/US 3) needles cast on 96 sts.
Work 7 rows in k1, p1 rib.
Inc row Rib 3, m1, rib 3, [m1, rib 2, m1, rib 3] to end. 133 sts.
Change to 4mm (No 8/US 6) needles.
Next row K1, [p1, k1] to end.
The last row forms moss st. Cont in moss st until work measures 11cm/4¼in from beg.
Dec row [Moss st 19, p3 tog] to last st, moss st 1.
Moss st 1 row.
Dec row [Moss st 17, p3 tog] to last st, moss st 1.
Moss st 1 row.
Dec row [Moss st 15, p3 tog] to last st, moss st 1.
Cont in this way, dec 12 sts as set on every alt row until 13 sts rem.
Break off yarn, thread end through rem sts, pull up and secure.
Join seam.

Cable Coat with Hat

See Page
37

MATERIALS
Coat 5 100g hanks of Rowan Recycled Chunky.
Pair each of 5mm (No 6/US 8) and 6mm (No 4/US 10) knitting needles.
Cable needle.
Crochet hook.
8 buttons.
Hat 1 100g hank of Rowan Recycled Chunky.
Pair of 6mm (No 4/US 10) knitting needles.
Cable needle.
Crochet hook.

TENSION
13 sts and 22 rows to 10cm/4in square over moss st on 6mm (No 4/US 10) needles.

MEASUREMENTS
To fit age	2-4	years
Actual chest	78	cm
measurement	30¾	in
Length	47	cm
	18½	in
Sleeve seam	24	cm
	9½	in

ABBREVIATIONS
C2B = sl next st onto cable needle and leave at back of work, k1, then k1 from cable needle;
C2F = sl next st onto cable needle and leave at front of work, k1, then k1 from cable needle.
Also see page 7.

CABLE PANEL
Worked over 10 sts.
1st row (wrong side) K2, p6, k2.
2nd row P2, k1, C2B, C2F, k1, p2.
3rd row K2, p6, k2.
4th row P2, C2B, k2, C2F, p2.
These 4 rows form patt.

Coat

BACK
With 6mm (No 4/US 10) needles cast on 78 sts.
1st row (wrong side) * [P1, k1] 4 times, work 1st row of cable panel; rep from * once, [p1, k1] 3 times, ** work 1st row of cable panel, [p1, k1] 4 times; rep from ** once.
2nd row * [K1, p1] 4 times, work 2nd row of cable panel; rep from * once, [k1, p1] 3 times, ** work 2nd row of cable panel, [k1, p1] 4 times; rep from ** once.
These 2 rows set position of panels and form moss st between panels. Patt 9 rows more.
Dec row Patt 6, work 2 tog, patt 16, work 2 tog, patt 26, work 2 tog, patt 16, work 2 tog, patt 6.
Patt 11 rows.
Dec row Patt 5, work 2 tog, patt 15, work 2 tog, patt 26, work 2 tog, patt 15, work 2 tog, patt 5.
Patt 11 rows.
Dec row Patt 4, work 2 tog, patt 14, work 2 tog, patt 26, work 2 tog, patt 14, work 2 tog, patt 4.
Patt 11 rows.
Dec row Patt 3, work 2 tog, patt 13, work 2 tog, patt 26, work 2 tog, patt 13, work 2 tog, patt 3. 62 sts.
Cont straight until Back measures 30cm/11¾in from beg, ending with a wrong side row.
Shape Armholes
Keeping patt correct, cast off 4 sts at beg of next 2 rows. 54 sts. Cont straight until Back measures 47cm/11½ in from beg, ending with a wrong side row.
Shape Shoulders
Cast off 9 sts at beg of next 4 rows.
Leave rem 18 sts on a holder.

LEFT FRONT
With 6mm (No 4/US 10) needles cast on 40 sts.
1st row (wrong side) [P1, k1] twice, * work 1st row of cable panel, [p1, k1] 4 times; rep from * once.
2nd row * [K1, p1] 4 times, work 2nd row of cable panel; rep from * once, [k1, p1] twice.
These 2 rows set position of panels and form moss st between panels. Patt 9 rows more.
Dec row Patt 6, work 2 tog, patt 16, work 2 tog, patt 14.
Patt 11 rows.
Dec row Patt 5, work 2 tog, patt 15, work 2 tog, patt 14.
Patt 11 rows.
Dec row Patt 4, [work 2 tog, patt 14]

twice.
Patt 11 rows.
Dec row Patt 3, work 2 tog, patt 13, work 2 tog, patt 14. 32 sts.
Cont straight until Front matches Back to armhole shaping, ending with a wrong side row.
Shape Armhole
Cast off 4 sts at beg of next row. 28 sts.
Cont straight until Front measures 41cm/16in from beg, ending with a wrong side row.
Shape Neck
Next row Patt to last 4 sts, turn; leave the 4 sts on a safety pin.
Dec one st at neck edge on next 4 rows then on 2 foll alt rows. 18 sts. Cont straight until Front matches Back to shoulder shaping, ending with a wrong side row.
Shape Shoulder
Cast off 9 sts at beg of next row. Work 1 row. Cast off rem 9 sts.
Mark front edge to indicate position of 6 buttons: first one 3 rows up from cast on edge, last one 1cm/¼in below neck shaping and rem 4 evenly spaced between.

RIGHT FRONT
With 6mm (No 4/US 10) needles cast on 40 sts.
1st row (wrong side) * [P1, k1] 4 times, work 1st row of cable panel; rep from * once, [p1, k1] twice.
2nd row [K1, p1] twice, * work 2nd row of cable panel, [k1, p1] 4 times; rep from * once.
These 2 rows set position of panels and form moss st between panels. Patt 1 row.
Buttonhole row Moss st 2, yrn, p2 tog, patt to end.
Making buttonholes to match markers on Left Front, cont as follows: patt 7 rows.
Dec row Patt 14, work 2 tog, patt 16, work 2 tog, patt 6.
Patt 11 rows.
Dec row Patt 14, work 2 tog, patt 15, work 2 tog, patt 5.
Patt 11 rows.
Dec row [Patt 14, work 2 tog] twice, patt 4.
Patt 11 rows.
Dec row Patt 14, work 2 tog, patt 13, work 2 tog, patt 3. 32 sts.
Complete to match Left Front, reversing shapings.

SLEEVES

With 6mm (No 4/US 10) needles cast on 38 sts.

1st row (wrong side) [P1, k1] 3 times, *work 1st row of cable panel, [p1, k1] 3 times; rep from * once.

2nd row [K1, p1] 3 times, * work 2nd row of cable panel, [k1, p1] 3 times; rep from * once.

These 2 rows set position of panels and form moss st between panels. Cont in patt, inc one st at each end of 2nd row and every foll 6th row until there are 54 sts, working inc sts into moss st. Cont straight until Sleeve measures 26cm/10¼in from beg, ending with a wrong side row. Cast off.

COLLAR

Join shoulder seams.

With 5mm (No 6/US 8) needles and right side facing, slip 4 sts from Right Front safety pin onto needle, pick up and k14 sts up right front neck, k back neck sts, pick up and k14 sts down left front neck, then moss st across 4 sts from safety pin. 54 sts. Moss st 1 row.

Next 2 rows Moss st to last 16 sts, turn.
Next 2 rows Moss st to last 14 sts, turn.
Next 2 rows Moss st to last 12 sts, turn.
Next 2 rows Moss st to last 10 sts, turn.
Next row Moss st to end.

Cast off 3 sts at beg of next 2 rows. Moss st 6 rows. Dec one st at each end of next 6 rows. Cast off 3 sts at beg of next 4 rows. Cast off loosely rem sts.

BELT

With 5mm (No 6/US 8) needles cast on 7 sts.

1st row K1, [p1, k1] to end.
Rep this row until belt measures 30cm/11¾in. Cast off.

TO MAKE UP

Sew on sleeves, placing centre of sleeves to shoulder seams and sewing ends of last 6 rows of sleeve tops to cast off sts at armholes. Join side and sleeve seams. Place belt on back where desired and secure each end in position with button. Sew on buttons. With crochet hook, make chain cord approximately 90cm/35½in long. Make 2 pom-poms and attach one to each end of cord. Place cord under collar and secure in position at back neckband and at each side of front bands.

Hat

With 6mm (No 4/US 10) needles cast on 72 sts.

1st row (wrong side) [P1, k1] twice, * work 1st row of cable panel, [p1, k1] 4 times; rep from * twice, work 1st row of cable panel, [p1, k1] twice.

2nd row [K1, p1] twice, * work 2nd row of cable panel, [k1, p1] 4 times; rep from * twice, work 2nd row of cable panel, [k1, p1] twice.

These 2 rows set position of panels and form moss st between panels. Cont in patt until work measures 16cm/6¼in from beg, ending with a wrong side row.

Dec row Patt 2, work 2 tog, [patt 10, work 2 tog, patt 4, work 2 tog] 3 times, patt 10, work 2 tog, patt 2.
Patt 1 row.

Dec row Patt 1, work 2 tog, [patt 10, work 2 tog, patt 2, work 2 tog] 3 times, patt 10, work 2 tog, patt 1. 56 sts.

Eyelet row Patt 1, [yrn, work 2 tog, patt 2] to last 3 sts, yrn, work 2 tog, patt 1.

Inc row Patt 2, m1, [patt 10, m1, patt 4, m1] 3 times, patt 10, m1, patt 2. 64 sts.
Working inc sts into moss st, patt 7 rows more. Cast off in patt.

Join back seam. With crochet hook, make chain cord approximately 32cm/12½in long. Thread through eyelet holes, pull up and tie into a bow. Make 2 pom-poms and attach one to each end of cord.

Yarn Source Guide

Rowan Yarn Addresses
Rowan Yarns are widely available in yarn shops. For details of stockists and mail order sources of Rowan Yarns, please write or contact the distributors listed below.
For advice on how to use a substitute yarn, see page 7

UNITED KINGDOM
Rowan Yarns,
Green Lane Mill, Holmfirth,
West Yorkshire, England
HD7 1RW
Tel: (01484) 681 881

USA
Westminster Trading Corporation,
5 Northern Boulevard, Amherst,
NH 03031
Tel: (603) 886 5041/5043

AUSTRALIA
Rowan (Australia),
191 Canterbury Road,
Canterbury, Victoria 3126
Tel: (03) 830 1609

BELGIUM
Hedera,
Pleinstraat 68,
3001 Leuven
Tel: (016) 23 21 89

CANADA
Estelle Designs & Sales Ltd,
Unit 65 & 67, 2220 Midland Avenue,
Scarborough, Ontario, M10 3E6
Tel: (416) 298 9922

DENMARK
Designer Garn,
Vesterbro 33 A,
DK-9000, Aalborg
Tel: (8) 98 13 48 24

FRANCE
Elle Tricote,
52 Rue Principale,
67300 Schiltigheim
Tel: (33) 88 62 65 31

GERMANY
Wolle + Design,
Wolfshover Strasse 76,
52428 Julich Stetternich
Tel: (49) 2461 54735

HOLLAND
Henk & Henrietta Beukers,
Dorpsstraat 9,
NL 5327 AR Hurwenen
Tel: (04182) 1764

ICELAND
Stockurinn,
Kjorgardi, Laugavegi 59,
ICE-101 Reykjavik
Tel: (01) 18254

ITALY
La Compagnia del Cotone,
Via Mazzini 44, I-10123 Torino
Tel: (011) 87 83 81

JAPAN
Diakeito Co Ltd,
2-3-11 Senba-Higashi, Minoh City,
Osaka 562
Tel: (0727) 27 6604

NEW ZEALAND
John Q Goldingham Ltd,
PO Box 45083, Epuni Railway,
Lower Hutt, Wellington, North Island
Tel: (04) 5674 085

NORWAY
Eureka,
PO Box 357, N-1401 Ski
Tel: (64) 86 55 70

SWEDEN
Wincent,
Sveavagen 94,
113 58 Stockholm
Tel: (08) 673 70 60

Author's Acknowledgments

I would like to thank the following knitters for their invaluable help - Pat Church, Connie Critchell, Janet Fagin, Jacqui Halstead, Shirley Kennet, and in particular Penny Hill for her tremendous support and for working such long hours!

I am extremely grateful to Tina Egleton for her hard work and patience when pattern checking, to Sandra Lousada for her beautiful photography and dedication to the task, and Marie Willey for her excellent styling and propping.

I would also like to thank Denise Bates, my wonderful editor, for creating the opportunity to work on this project, and Heather Jeeves, my agent, for doing such a brilliant job.